HOWARD DEAN

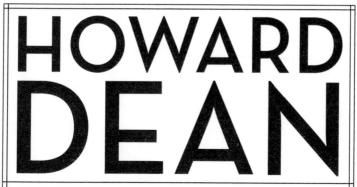

HOWARD DEAN

A Citizen's Guide to the Man Who Would Be President

By a team of reporters for Vermont's <u>Rutland Herald</u> & <u>Times-Argus</u>

Edited by Dirk Van Susteren

Steerforth Press
South Royalton, Vermont

For information about permission to reproduce
selections from this book, write to:
Steerforth Press, L.C., P.O. Box 70,
South Royalton, VT 05068

Library of Congress Cataloging-in-Publication Data

Howard Dean: a citizen's guide to the man who would be president /
by a team of reporters for Vermont's Times-Argus and Rutland Herald.
—1st ed.
    p.   cm.

ISBN 1-5864-2075-5 (alk. paper)
1. Dean, Howard, 1948– 2. Dean, Howard, 1948– — Political and
social views. 3. Presidential candidates — United States — Biography.
4. Governors — Vermont — Biography. 5. Presidents — United States
— Election — 2004. 6. United States — Politics and government —
2001–
7. Vermont — Politics and government — 20th century.
E840.8.D4 H68 2003
974.3'044'092–dc22
                                2003020684
FIRST EDITION

CONTENTS

EDITOR'S NOTE

In her book *Shrub,* a sassy look at the performance of George W. Bush when he was governor of Texas, columnist Molly Ivins suggests that inexperienced reporters be advised of the three ways to assess a politician. "The first is to look at the record. The second is to look at the record. And the third, look at the record."

Good advice, and that's what we have attempted to do with this book on Vermont's former governor Howard Dean — only we chose experienced reporters for the assignment, some of whom have covered Dean for years.

This book was a collaborative project. It involved three entities: The *Rutland Herald* and its sister paper, the *Barre-Montpelier Times-Argus*; Steerforth Press, a book publisher in South Royalton, Vermont, and a team of nine writers.

The three groups shook hands in early August 2003 when it became clear we had a good story on our hands. After a lackluster campaign start in spring, Howard Dean by mid-summer was stunning the political world with his ability to raise money and appeal to voters. In late July a political poll indicated this little-known governor from a small state was the top choice among likely voters in California's important Democratic primary. Dean's harsh criticism of President Bush's handling of the Iraq war and the U.S. economy was resonating. This book was completed in eight weeks.

Howard Dean — the citizen's guide — does not tell everything there is to know about Howard Dean. While governor for nearly 12 years, Dean was involved in many events and issues that earned him both criticism and praise. We have focused on those deemed most significant for Vermont and those that provide special insight into the former governor's personality and character.

We received much help with this book. Dean's personal acquaintances through the years and legislators and government officials who worked with him generously shared their observations. We thank them. We also give a hearty thank you to the writers' spouses. They endured much during the busy race toward deadline.

Dirk Van Susteren
October 2003

HOWARD
DEAN

INTRODUCTION

I got the call at home on the morning of August 14, 1991. Gov. Richard Snelling was dead. The *Rutland Herald* would publish an extra edition that afternoon, and I needed to get to work. For Vermonters, the shock of Snelling's death was considerable, and it was magnified by the uncertainty we felt about his successor. The question we were asking ourselves was an obvious one, but it gained new importance in those hours of shock and grief: Who is Howard Dean? It took the next decade for those of us in the press, and our readership, to gain an understanding of the energetic, ambitious politician who was sworn into office that summer afternoon in 1991. When Snelling died, Howard Dean was in his fifth year as lieutenant governor, and we were at least superficially acquainted with him, but we had little notion about the scope of Dean's ambitions or what kind of governor he would make.

Who is Howard Dean? Vermont is small enough that many Vermonters have the chance for personal encounters with their political leaders, and Howard Dean had already had a close encounter with a friend of mine. It was at a political gathering in Castleton, a small college town near the New York border, and my friend, a Congregational minister, fell unconscious from cardiac arrest. Dean, a physician, applied mouth-to-mouth resuscitation and kept my friend alive.

That was one thing we knew about Howard Dean. He was a physician who had a practice with his wife. In fact, he was seeing a patient when he learned that Snelling had died, and it was part of the lore of that historic moment that Dean finished his appointment with his patient before heading for Montpelier to become governor.

We knew also that he had come from a privileged background that included a childhood on Long Island, prep school and Yale. As a Democrat, he had risen quickly to a position of leadership in the Vermont House of Representatives, and then he ran successfully for lieutenant governor. As with most lieutenant governors, we presumed he had plans to run for governor. No one foresaw that he would claim that office so soon.

Who is Howard Dean? We learned quickly that he had an off-the-cuff manner and habit of frankness that led him to say things that were insensitive or brash. Over the years, the press chided him for his insensitivity and praised him for his candor. His candor seemed to arise from a brimming self-confidence and from a doctor's habit of giving the news straight. He did not agonize or apologize, and he relished the give-and-take with the press and the public.

Over time Dean's political profile began to take shape. After he was sworn in as governor, he declared his intention to stick with the economic recovery plan that Gov. Snelling, a Republican, had put in place the previous winter. Vermont state government was digging out from a deficit after the recession of the early 1990s, and Dean established from the outset a reputation for fiscal austerity.

He began to focus on some favorite initiatives, such as programs for children and families and health-care reform. He promoted land conservation, which won him praise from environmentalists, and he bemoaned excessive regulation, which won him praise from business. He mounted campaigns against drunken driving and drug addiction, and he gained a reputation as tough on crime.

Dean signed his name to two landmark bills during his tenure. One of them refashioned the state's system of education finance, eliminating disparities between revenues available from town to town. The other established civil unions, which gave gay and lesbian couples the same rights as married couples. Dean did not lead the way for either bill; the legislature passed the bills in response to rulings by the Vermont Supreme Court. But he supported both bills, and he did not back away from the controversies they created.

Over the course of 11 years in office, Dean's ambitions as

governor began to wane, and his attention began to shift to national politics. Those who followed his career began to sense that Vermont was no longer a large enough stage for him. We knew he had considered a presidential campaign in 2000, and when he announced after his election in 2002 that he would not seek re-election, we understood he had his sights on a presidential run in 2004.

It is an astonishing lesson in American politics to watch a political leader grow from a familiar local figure, someone known as a doctor, a youth-hockey coach, a governor, to a politician of national stature. Every word now spoken or written about him has a heightened importance, and the discussion of his history, personality and ideas takes place in a resounding echo chamber of intensified media scrutiny. That is because the stakes have become so high.

As that scrutiny has intensified, it seemed like a useful exercise to share with readers the perspective of the most experienced observers of the phenomenon of Howard Dean. We have gathered those observations together here. If readers in San Diego or Seattle or Tallahassee find the story of Dean's sudden rise curious and surprising, so do those who know him, though we also have an insight into how it all came about. Even before a single vote has been cast, Howard Dean's rise has become a remarkable story of ambition and accomplishment, of craft and luck. And it is a story worth telling now.

David Moats

Former Vermont governor Howard Dean
speaks to supporters at Habour Place
in Portsmouth, New Hampshire,
on July 22, 2003.
(AP Photo by Carrie Niland, Portsmouth Herald)

CHAPTER 1

From Out
of Nowhere

It was a puzzling scene, and if the tall fellow in the blue blazer was more flummoxed than most other folks, it wasn't by much.

There on a platform, a microphone sticking up in front of him, boats bobbing in Portsmouth Harbor in the late-afternoon summer sunlight behind him, was this little guy. Five-nine, tops, and looking smaller yet because he'd taken off his suit coat. Something about a little guy standing in a striped tie and a white shirt — with the sleeves rolled up, and the collar unbuttoned — makes him look . . . oh, let's say short on the gravitas.

Not a bad-looking guy, but no matinee idol. No great orator, either. A strong enough voice, but no distinctive timbre to it. Strong enough words, too, but without eloquence. "A campaign based on hope will always beat a campaign based on fear," in addition to being wrong, will not show up as Exhibit A in rhetoric class.

And yet, spread out before Howard Brush Dean — for it was he standing on that platform, uttering that less-than-deathless prose — were 600 people filling the plaza overlooking New Hampshire's only port. That's lots of folks on a weekday afternoon in July, seven months before they were going to vote for

Dean or for one of his opponents in their state's legendary, first-in-the-nation presidential primary.

They weren't just standing there, either. Just about every one of them was hanging on every word, applauding every sentence, and growing close to ecstatic just by being in the presence of their hero.

And all for one reason: He was really sticking it to George W. Bush.

"This president played the race card," Dean said, and the crowd roared. "Your property taxes go up so he can send tax cuts to his friends like Ken Lay," he said, and the plaza seemed to shake.

They nodded when he said, "Each one of us is responsible to make sure that every child has health insurance." They laughed and clapped when he said, "Democrats are almost as angry at the Democratic Party in Washington as they are at George Bush." And they screamed their approval when he said, "The way to beat George Bush is not to be a little bit like him."

A puzzling scene indeed, considering that half of these folks had probably never heard of Howard Dean just a few months earlier, and apparently a mystery to the tall television correspondent in the blue blazer, who was trying to formulate the question by which the mystery might be solved.

"How can the liberal former governor of Vermont, a supporter of gay rights . . ." the fellow said, aloud, into his microphone, indifferent to annoying the people nearby. Standing two feet from his cameraman, atop a two-foot-high brick wall enclosing a flowerbed, Blue-blazer tried again.

"Can a liberal former governor of Vermont, a supporter of gay marriage, threaten to capture the Democratic nomination? . . ."

Whereupon he stopped again, perhaps realizing that Dean does not support gay marriage.

"If being liberal means balancing the budget, call me a liberal," Dean was saying. Behind him, just upstream of the bridge to Kittery, Maine, wobbled a pleasure boat sporting a "Dean for President" sign. Again the crowd roared its approval of his words, and Blue-blazer, indifferent to the animosity developing around him, tried again: "How can a liberal governor of Vermont who supports gay rights win the Democratic presidential nomination in George Bush's America? This is Blue-blazer McPhee for the BBC with the Dean campaign in Portsmouth, New Hampshire."

The BBC? And you thought the Brits were polite.

Say this for Blue-blazer. He may not have been much more accurate than he was courteous, but he almost got the question right. And seeing as he's a foreigner, we can forgive him for the almost part, for in truth the scene before him was close to inexplicable. So, come to think of it, is the simple fact that Howard Dean really is threatening to capture the Democratic presidential nomination, and he's doing it by breaking the rules.

If Blue-blazer really understood the situation, he'd have put it this way: How did this unimposing, little-known fellow with a reedy voice and a bland speaking style who comes from a tiny state as famous for its political kookiness as its maple syrup get to where he might become president of the United States?

After all, Democratic insiders laughed back in May 2002 when Dean said he would run for president. He had no money, no name recognition, no charisma. By Labor Day 2003, he was the front-runner, and those same Democrats were wondering whether anything or anybody could stop him.

Two weeks later, some of those Democrats had a plan — and a candidate — to stop him. But the entry of retired Gen. Wesley Clark into the race served to underscore Dean's accomplishment; he was the only one of the nine pre-Clark candidates who had excited the voters. Nobody else had gotten 600 apparently sane Democrats to Portsmouth in July.

"This period before the Iowa caucuses is the real first primary, or some call it the invisible primary. He's won it," says Mark Siegel, a former executive director of the Democratic National Committee and a generally acknowledged expert on the party's nominating process. "He's got the buzz, and nobody has yet voted."

But he didn't just have the buzz. He had the whole political world in a tizzy. Mostly the Democrats, to be sure, but some Republicans, too.

"There is something going on there," veteran New Hampshire Republican strategist Tom Rath told *USA Today,* "and I tell you, if we don't pay attention . . . we're making a big mistake."

The Dean surge did not simply discombobulate the political world; it turned it upside down and put it into high-speed over-drive. The Anybody-But-The-Front-Runner movement that traditionally arises after the first round of primaries blossomed in September. In this case it was Anybody But Dean, and the Anybody was Clark, who, despite a less-than-impressive debut, challenged Dean's front-runner position in some of the polls.

But Clark's mid-September enlistment into the candidate ranks, supported as it was by several congressmen, consultants, columnists and associates of Bill Clinton, was just another sign of how deeply Dean had discomfited the pros. It wasn't that Clark's candidacy was the creation of conspirators in a smoke-filled room. Nor, despite a plethora of political drivel in print and on the morning TV shows, was Clark any kind of "stalking horse" for Sen. Hillary Clinton. Stalking horses went out with high-button shoes. But the speed with which so many Democratic pros flocked to Clark demonstrated how surprised they were by Dean's success. From the perspective of pure drama, the Dean fad was an uncommonly good show; what's better theater than the discomfiture of the establishment?

> "This period before the Iowa caucuses is the real first primary, or some call it the invisible primary. He's won it."
>
> Mark Siegel,
> Former Executive Director of the
> Democratic National Committee

So Blue-blazer was asking (if imprecisely) the obvious question: How did this happen?

Half the answer was right in front of him, where a Democrat

was attacking the Republican president. Really attacking him — condemning his policies, ridiculing his intellect, even questioning his integrity. Doing, in short, all those things that prudent political practitioners, consultants, and commentators warned Democrats not to do.

Caution seemed like pretty good advice at the time. For awhile there George Bush wasn't just a popular president; he was a political colossus. Beyond his high approval ratings was the perception that any criticism of him appeared downright disreputable.

It helped that part of the media — most talk radio and some cable television — acted less as independent observers than as a Republican Party auxiliary, and that the mainstream news outlets were hardly aggressive toward the administration. The few liberal commentators flying the anti-Bush banner might as well have been shouting into the wind. On the surface, at least, it seemed as if Blue-blazer had it right: This was "George Bush's America."

Maybe Burlington, Vermont, is too far from conventional wisdom, or maybe Howard Dean knew that beyond the Beltway and outside the scope of the consultants and the professional chatterers, something was bubbling. In the wise words of that daily political dope sheet *The Note* from ABC News, "Practicing and covering nomination politics are imperfect sciences, but you really can learn something about the mood of a party and — we are serious — about the mood of the nation, when an insurgent candidate does well."

What we learned was that there was and is fierce opposition to George Bush. Those polls did not lie; Bush was popular. But there was a hefty minority — perhaps 40 percent of the voters — who had not embraced him. Throughout his presidency, some 38 percent of the people kept telling the *New York Times*–CBS News Poll that they still weren't convinced Bush had won the 2000 election fair and square.

Who were these dissidents? Democrats, for the most part, precisely the folks who vote in Democratic primaries and attend Democratic caucuses — the very people who will choose the

Democratic nominee. And many of them did not simply "not-love" Bush. They disliked him with an intensity that (usually) stopped just short of hate.

Though this opposition was not small, it was, to modify a phrase from Richard Nixon, a silenced minority. Thanks to that near-consensus among the political cognoscenti that Bush was Superman, dissenters were cowed. "Certain kinds of criticism have been largely banished from mainstream discourse," complained Jonathan Chait, a liberal writer, but one who had supported Bush on the Iraq war. Expressing anti-Bush sentiments became almost an underground ritual. Couples in the safety of their living rooms, co-workers at lunch away from their (presumably) fierce pro-Bush colleagues, now and then strangers in a bar or airport catching signals from one another that they were . . . well, different.

So when someone finally came along and really lit into the president, the reaction transcended the political. It was a shock of recognition, rather like the response of millions of women when feminism reappeared in the early '70s — "Oh! I thought I was the only one who felt that way, and here is someone saying it out loud." That Dean first said it about the war with Iraq only magnified the reaction, because it was over the war that the fervor of the pro-Bush media and the deference of the mainstream press most blatantly conspired to create the impression that dissent was treasonous.

Dean would have none of that. His breakthrough came when all the presidential candidates spoke to the winter meeting of the Democratic National Committee. All the others opened calmly, smiling for the cameras and thanking their hosts. Not Dean, who strode to the podium and blurted out, "What I want to know is why so many Democrats in Washington aren't standing up against Bush's unilateral war in Iraq. My name is Howard Dean, and I represent the Democratic wing of the Democratic Party."

It was electrifying, not just to the Dean supporters but to neutral observers such as Democratic political strategist Elaine Kamarck. "It was dynamite," she says.

Once again, the pundits got it wrong. Immediately Dean became "the anti-war candidate" and therefore — a drum role here — a "liberal," if not the candidate of "the Left." Well, he was against the war, and that opposition did appeal to the folks who had gone to peace marches and pasted "No War with Iraq" bumper stickers on their cars.

But if they were the only Dean supporters, he wouldn't be a potential nominee. It was less his opposition to the war than his opposition to Bush that attracted so many frustrated Democrats, including some who didn't agree with him on the war.

There is nothing new about this. Americans have always been drawn to a candidate who speaks his mind even if they disagree with what he is saying. Otherwise Ronald Reagan wouldn't have been elected. People like a candidate who is (or at least seems to be) authentically himself, not a creature of political professionals who warn their bosses to keep quiet until the results of the latest poll have been analyzed. That's how Dean came across to Democrats who were waiting for somebody — anybody — to take on Bush.

And to take on the Democrats who wouldn't. One reason Democrats did so poorly in the 2002 mid-term elections was that their leaders were afraid to attack the president. They carefully calibrated their positions, hoping that if they supported a slightly smaller tax cut, a slightly larger prescription drug benefit, and showed just a little less eagerness to go to war, they could eke out just enough votes from their core constituencies to keep control of the Senate and take over the House of Representatives. They didn't. They just frustrated rank-and-file Democrats.

> It was less his opposition to the war than his opposition to Bush that attracted so many frustrated Democrats, including some who didn't agree with Dean on the war.

Not only was Dean forthright, he was forthright in plain

English. Dean really is something of a policy wonk, one of those people who reads every word of the news section of the *New York Times.* In a meeting of government officials, he can talk government jargon with the best of them. But he knows better than to talk that way on the stump.

"Dean is like Clinton. He can talk about policy without making it boring," says Kamarck.

He can even talk about it just a touch naughtily. On July 5, 2003, at a house party in New Hampshire, Dean told the 100 or so folks in attendance that public policy should not be affected because Bush "has a Jones for oil." The crowd was both surprised and delighted. To "have a Jones," according to the Online Slang Dictionary, means to have an intense craving, perhaps for a drug, perhaps for something else. Verging just slightly on the bawdy, this is not the way presidential candidates usually talk. It is, however, the way people in the backyard of a neighbor's house often talk, and apparently it's the way Howard Dean sometimes talks. Some voters, at least, seem to like it.

But some do not. Neither do some political Pooh-bahs. It is their antipathy — not just to the slang, but to the entire Dean approach — that stands between Dean and the Democratic nomination as much as the other contenders.

Blue-blazer voiced only one of the two pertinent questions, asking how Dean got where he is. The second is if he can go further, to the nomination and the presidency, and the answer to that one is more complicated, because he faces institutional adversaries as well as competing candidates.

> In Howard Dean's case, the adversaries are the Democratic Party subdivision of that establishment, and the aggressive but sometimes petty national political press corps.

They are intertwined, these institutional adversaries, and though they hardly constitute a conspiracy, they do place extra obstacles in the path of the insurgent candidate.

In Dean's case, the adversaries are the Democratic Party subdivision of that establishment, and the aggressive but sometimes petty national political press corps. The obstacles they have placed in his path are the perception of him as "liberal," and therefore likely to be crushed by Bush as George McGovern was crushed by Richard Nixon in 1972, and the suggestion that he "flip-flops," changes his position on some issues.

To understand the nature of these adversaries and the potency of the obstacles, two short digressions are necessary to answer two questions: What is the political establishment? And what is a liberal?

BUCKING THE ESTABLISHMENT

A decade ago, during Bill Clinton's troubled first year as president, *Washington Post* writer Sally Quinn tried to explain that many of her friends disliked the president because they felt he had insufficiently appreciated them. "People who have been here and who have attained a certain social or political position do not want to be 'dissed,'" she wrote. "They want the new team to respect them. Because these tribal rituals were not fulfilled, many people were virtually gleeful when Clinton went into a free fall in the polls."

For at least the last three decades, the talk and the style of Washington have been dominated by a permanent corps of successful political operatives, lobbyists and journalists. If they are in different professions, they are essentially in the same business. The Republicans and Democrats among them may disagree, but they socialize together and protect one another. As noted by Quinn, their quasi-official chronicler, they constitute a tribe.

It is important to recognize this phenomenon, but there is no point in lamenting it. Human beings are tribal by nature, and people with similar interests flock together. This tribe sees itself as playing a nationally important role; if it is not exactly the permanent government, it is the permanent government's monitor. It influences (though it does not control) the professionals in both political parties, the political think tanks that place their policy experts on the TV chat shows, and the media, especially the opinion columnists. It does not like Howard Dean.

Not that it is as hostile to him as it was to Clinton, whom it saw as a rube. Clinton may have been a Rhodes Scholar and Yale Law School graduate, but to Washington insiders he was an unsophisticated rural Arkansan, as Jimmy Carter had been an unsophisticated rural Georgian. (Though many in the Washington establishment have Southern roots, a certain condescension toward Southerners permeates it.) Dean is a physician, a New Yorker, the son and grandson of Wall Street brokers. But he is not in the tribe, which prefers, as do all tribes, one of its own, or at least someone it knows. It knows five of Dean's opponents pretty well — four senators and a senior congressman.

The very senators and congressman Dean disparaged in his speeches — three of the senators and the congressman for supporting the Iraq war, the fourth senator, Bob Graham of Florida, for having little chance of getting nominated. Graham's prospects aren't good, but Dean broke a tribal code by saying so. To make matters worse, most of the tribe supported the Iraq war or dissented gently, with much deference to the president and his advisers. Dean excoriated the war, perhaps another code violation.

Dean criticizes, sometimes harshly, sometimes with a touch of the snide. The establishment tribe does not approve of these manners, especially when exhibited by Democrats. Incivility from House Majority Leader Tom DeLay or radioman Rush Limbaugh gets more leeway, perhaps because they simply ignore criticism. The establishment is harder on liberals because most of it is mildly liberal, whatever that may be.

WHAT IS A LIBERAL?

A liberal may be defined by a set of public policy positions. As such, a liberal is someone who believes in racial and sexual equality, favors gay rights, thinks a woman ought to have the right to choose an abortion, believes that everyone should have health insurance and that Social Security and Medicare ought to be kept essentially as they are, espouses stronger gun control laws, wants tougher environmental regulations and more land preserved in its wild state, favors a progressive income tax and raising the minimum wage from time to time, wants a strong public school system staffed by better-paid teachers, favors free trade but with more protections for labor and the environment, and believes that when the United States acts abroad it should do so with the cooperation of its allies and under the auspices of the United Nations.

That mostly describes Howard Dean. But there's something else it describes: most Americans. A passel of polls, taken over the years, leaves little doubt that all the policy positions listed above would be embraced by a majority of the people, some by a large majority. There are issues on which Americans are conservative. Most people oppose gay marriage. The more generous welfare program repealed in 1996 was unpopular, as is affirmative action. Most voters favor the death penalty, and few oppose lower taxes.

Unless the alternative to lower taxes is shoring up Social Security and Medicare, improving the schools, cleaning the air, or balancing the budget. Then a majority would forego tax cuts. By and large, liberalism is what the folks in academia would call the dominant paradigm.

And yet, in the same polls that reflect those liberal opinions, only about 20 percent of the people describe themselves as liberals. That's because the word "liberal" has come to mean less a set of policy positions than a set of attitudes, even a set of consumer preferences. A "liberal" these days is less someone who cares about the working class than someone who listens to National Public Radio and drives a Volvo. Someone, in short, who is . . . well, different from the average American, less likely to go to church or watch Monday Night Football. As it happens, most Americans do not go to church or watch Monday Night Football, but accuracy is irrelevant here; it's the vibes that matter.

Worse, from the liberal perspective, is the fact that a combination of conservative cleverness and liberal obtuseness has created the impression that a liberal is someone who is not tough enough. Subtly, and sometimes not so subtly, there is the hint that liberals are effeminate. It should not be surprising that over the last 25 years, women have voted increasingly for liberal candidates while men have become more conservative.

Besides, liberals are the folks who keep telling the rest of us that we're not living right. It was liberals who told Americans that they were wrong to discriminate by race or gender. Most Americans now agree, but a vestigial bitterness lingers, more personal than political, against those who brought those messages. They effectively insulted the parents and grandparents of Southerners (and not only Southerners) whose cherished "way of life" depended on segregation, and everybody's mother and grandmother who had stayed home to tend the kids while Dad and Grandpa went off to work.

They're still at it. From the political left come the warnings that the food we eat is bad for us and the way we produce it bad for the land and water, that bigger is not necessarily better, that shopping 'til you drop may be unsustainable on a crowded, finite planet. And they sometimes do it in a school-marmish manner, enhancing that effeminant reputation: Fasten your seatbelts. Don't smoke. Eat less beef and more whole grains. Ditch that SUV for a fuel-efficient compact. They don't quite add "Eat your spinach," but sometimes they come close. Not long from now, majorities may agree that these scolds were right after all, as were the advocates of racial and sexual equality. But telling folks they don't live right is not the road to popularity, even if it turns out that you were correct.

The divide between liberalism as a set of public policy opinions and liberalism as the way you strut your stuff is obvious in how the conventional wisdom — well, the conventional outlook — holds that Dean and Sen. John Kerry of Massachusetts are the liberals in the Democratic race, while Gen. Clark, Sen. Graham, Sen. John Edwards of North Carolina and Rep. Dick Gephardt of Missouri are the moderates. On the record of their public policy positions, Gephardt is to Dean's left. But he's from Missouri, not Vermont. He's a church-going Catholic while

Dean rarely attends services. Gephardt didn't sign a civil unions bill.

On the surface, Dean would seem easily painted as a haughty, wine-and-cheese liberal, even though he has had no alcoholic beverage for more than 20 years. That's part of his problem. He doesn't drink at all. He wasn't in the armed services. He opposed the war with Iraq. He goes biking and canoeing for fun. He signed that civil unions bill giving same-sex couples the functional equivalent of marriage.

> Still, Vermont's reputation cooperates with image-makers who want to imply that a politician from the state is just a little different, too receptive to wacky ideas, perhaps not tough enough to be president.

And he's from a state that most Americans would love to visit, as long as their children don't decide to stay there to join a back-to-the-land commune where they would grow organic vegetables, wear Birkenstocks, drive a Volvo and vote for the state's lone and nominally socialist congressman.

It is politically irrelevant that this describes a Vermont that does not exist. That back-to-the-land influx petered out 25 years ago; its participants either returned to Scarsdale or stayed to fit in with the locals, perhaps driving Volvos, but just as likely pickup trucks. Volvos are expensive, after all. With a Republican governor, one independent senator and a split state legislature, the state is less reliably Democratic than California. And if Rep. Bernie Sanders is to the left of most Americans — and of Howard Dean — he hasn't spoken a distinctively socialist word in years.

Still, Vermont's reputation cooperates with image-makers who want to imply that a politician from the state is just a little different, too receptive to wacky ideas, perhaps not tough enough to be president.

This is one of Howard Dean's dilemmas — how to convince Middle America that he is not a strange duck, not weak, not too far to the left. It is an ironic dilemma, because whatever else Dean may be, he is tough, he is a middlebrow who has lived his life according to the accepted norms, and he is not very far to the left on the ideological spectrum. He is to the left of George W. Bush, but so is every Democrat. Within the Democratic Party, Dean is slightly right of center. For a liberal, he's pretty conservative.

Otherwise, he would not have come into politics as a supporter of Jimmy Carter, who was being challenged from his party's left by Sen. Edward Kennedy in 1980.

"The Carter people were older, sort of the party establishment," says Dean, who was a Carter-pledged delegate at the Democratic National Convention. "I was only about 30. The Kennedy people were younger. I voted all day with the Carter people and partied all night with the Kennedy people."

So, soon thereafter when an opening occurred for the Democratic chairmanship of Chittenden County, which includes the Vermont's largest city, Burlington, party leaders turned to young Doctor Dean. He told them he hardly knew anybody, but they said, he recalls, "Well, for some reason we don't understand, you're the only person who can get along with the Carter people and the Kennedy people."

Which may well have been what he had in mind — ingratiating himself with both factions so he could begin a political career. But it is significant that he chose to begin it as a moderate, fighting the party's liberal wing.

And he rarely misses the chance to remind voters that, unlike most liberal Democrats, he supported the first President Bush's Gulf War in 1991, as well as the 2001 invasion of Afghanistan. "We have the right to strike anybody in self-defense," he says. "We have a right to stop attacks."

But, say the anti-Dean Democrats, even if Dean is not really too liberal, he is too easily painted as too liberal to have a chance against George W. Bush. A primary vote for Dean, they say, is a step toward a general election debacle.

"To win the White House, the threshold issue is whether the American people come to believe the Democratic candidate will keep the country safe," says Al From, chief executive officer of the Democratic Leadership Council, formed in the 1980s to counter the party's domination by left-of-center interest groups. "I personally believe that it will be hard for any Democrat who didn't support the war, particularly someone not strong on the military, to win the White House in 2004."

From made those remarks before the post-war situation in Iraq began to deteriorate enough to make many Americans question the whole enterprise. And Dean disputes the assumption that voters doubt his commitment to national security. When asked how he could allay the average person's concerns that he might not be strong enough to be president, he shot back, "I don't think the average person has any such concern."

What the anti-Dean Democrats are hoping is that many in their rank-and-file will put pragmatism above preference, that they will say to themselves: "I prefer Dean, but Clark (or Kerry or Lieberman, etc.) is OK, too, and someone other than Dean will have a better chance in the fall."

Recent history does not bode well for such a wish. For at least the past 25 years, primary voters have chosen the contenders they like, whether or not they think he could win in the general election. People vote for candidates they like. They don't vote for a candidate because he or she fits into some party strategy. The Democratic Party as a corporate entity that determines who will be its presidential candidate does not exist. The primary and caucus voters determine that.

Still, if Dean has to slog it out in the February and March primaries, the establishment's opposition could hurt him, especially because of the "front-loaded" political calendar. Back in 1976, when Carter did what Dean is trying to do, half the convention delegates weren't selected until 11 weeks after the New Hampshire primary. That gave Carter time to build on his win in New Hampshire, raise money, build organizations in the next primary states, and court both the politicians and the leaders of Democratic-leaning interest groups.

This time everything is bunched up. This nomination will almost certainly be won by March 9, six weeks after the New Hampshire primary. By that night, almost two-thirds of the pledged delegates to the Democratic convention will have been selected. Not much time to raise money, make nice with the mayor, take the state chairman to dinner. An advantage, then, to the candidate with the big-name backing. The candidate who has the support of the governor, the mayor, the labor unions, already has an army of volunteers to hand out brochures, stack the studio audience at the TV debate and get out the vote.

Dean's plan is not to slog it out. His plan is to ride The Wave. That's political jargon for becoming a phenomenon, for arousing enough enthusiasm among enough voters to achieve celebrity status and an aura of inevitability about your nomination, if not your election.

Ironically, the bunched-up political calendar, designed precisely to allow a front-runner — presumably an establishment favorite — to wrap up the nomination, helps any candidate who can ride The Wave, even an insurgent. So Dean might trump the insiders at their own game.

But the game will not only end earlier than ever; it has started earlier than ever. Partly that's because of the early primaries. But mostly it's because of the culture — 24-hour news programs, constant (and often ill-informed) commentary by Internet "bloggers," the decadent confluence of politics and entertainment all combine to give the campaign a structure long before anyone cast a vote.

> Because Vermont still has moderate Republicans, politics in the state remains uncommonly civil. And the whole state is rather like a small town.

So Dean was already riding The Wave in July. The place to be, of course, but a precarious spot. He who rides The Wave is the target, not just of his opponents and the establishment bigwigs but also of political reporters, who, it seems, love nothing better than to put an insurgent candidate on that surfboard atop the swell and then dump him into the breakers.

This, too, started earlier than ever, and at first Dean didn't quite know how to respond. It was new to him, and to explain why, another short digression is required.

TOUGHER TREATMENT

When she ran for governor against Dean in 1998, Republican Ruth Dwyer made a speech in St. Johnsbury, in Vermont's "Northeast Kingdom," where she said that the state's unemployment rate was low only because so many Vermonters worked across the Connecticut River in New Hampshire.

She offered no evidence for this assertion, there being none, and none of the reporters covering the speech asked her for any then or later. It wouldn't be the Vermont way. There are many able reporters in the state, but aggressive questioning is not in their nature. It seems almost a sign of ill breeding. Because Vermont still has moderate Republicans, politics in the state remains uncommonly civil. And the whole state is rather like a small town; a reporter is likely to see in the restaurant in the evening the politician he or she raked over the coals that morning. With a few exceptions, Vermont's journalists tend to be gentle. That's what Dean was used to.

Welcome to the NFL. Some national political reporters love nothing better than to catch politicians using different words on Thursday to make the same point they did on Monday, or — worse yet — altering their position on some issue. Such behavior is scorned as a "flip-flop" and regarded as a sure sign that the candidate is flighty, if not downright dishonest.

Though often petty, the tactic has its uses. It can expose a charlatan, and it can keep a candidate mentally nimble. Dean, though no charlatan, was at first less than nimble, denying, for instance, that he had ever spoken favorably about the idea of raising the Social Security retirement age. He must have thought he was in Vermont, where reporters were less likely to check old transcripts.

Then he stumbled into the Middle East thicket. Dean is unscripted; he speaks spontaneously. This is a strength; voters see it as candor. But it got him into trouble when he told a New Mexico audience that the United States should not "take sides" in negotiations between Palestinians and Israelis, and that an "enormous number" of Israel's West Bank settlements would have to be dismantled eventually.

Taken literally, nothing in that statement offends longstanding U.S. policy, or majority public opinion on Israel. But certain phrases have political resonance. Not to "take sides" sounded a little like being "evenhanded," an old phrase that once meant granting bona fides even to the Palestinian hard-liners who seek nothing less than Israel's dissolution.

Dean, whose wife and children are Jewish, meant nothing of the sort. But — rookie mistake — he did not realize how his political opponents in both parties would jump on his wording. As he said a few days later, he would have to learn to use "different euphemisms."

He would also have to acknowledge that he has changed his mind about some issues. Most people do, of course, but political reporters, properly, wonder whether some changes are sincere or merely an effort to appeal to an interest group, a practice they revile as "pandering." Dean has changed his mind to some extent about free trade. He is not alone, and there are reasons for such a change — the comparative costs and benefits of the trade treaties are open to debate — but it leaves him open to the charge that he is pandering to organized labor, an important constituency in Iowa.

That's where the official process begins on Martin Luther King Day, Monday evening, January 19, 2004, when hundreds of thousands of Democrats go to a church basement, high school auditorium or neighbor's living room to stand in a corner.

Not because they've misbehaved, but to indicate which candidate they favor. The Dean supporters will gather in one corner, Lieberman backers in another, and so on. Officially, they are only selecting delegates to the next level in a multistage process ending in a state convention that selects the delegates to the Democratic National Convention. But from those little knots of devoted Democrats, state party officials will be able to determine who won, and by how much, at which point the political journalists will interpret those results, informing the citizenry of the deeper significance of it all.

Having already won the invisible primary, Dean cannot afford to stumble in this first visible contest. He does not have to win it. Gephardt comes from a neighboring state and won Iowa in 1988. Coming in second to Gephardt would be an acceptable finish for Dean, as long as it is not a distant second. Because he was running even with Gephardt in the autumn Iowa polls, the interpreters would interpret anything less than a close second — much less finishing behind Clark — to mean that many voters had taken a second look, and found him wanting.

If Dean wins Iowa, he will be hard to stop. The New Hampshire primary is only eight days later, and if a New Englander upsets a Midwesterner in the Midwest, that New Englander roars into New Hampshire with what the older George Bush once called "The Big Mo" (a momentum squandered by that same Bush, who chose to talk about it instead of meaningful issues during the three weeks between winning Iowa and losing New Hampshire to Ronald Reagan). Theoretically, it is possible to win these first two contests and still not win your party's nomination. It has never happened.

"You've got to stop him in Iowa," says Elaine Kamarck, who was one of Al Gore's senior political advisers before teaching at Harvard's John F. Kennedy School of Government. "You can't let him have a twofer. If he takes the two of them, given that he's got money and he's running [TV] ads in so many states all over the country, I don't see how anybody can beat him."

New Hampshire, on January 27, comes close to being a must-win contest for both Dean and Kerry. It would be hard for either of them to argue that a loss there was anything other than a rejection by the neighbors. Should Dean lose New Hampshire, he would join John McCain, Gary Hart, Bruce Babbitt, John Anderson, and other presidential hopefuls who created a stir for a while and then became footnotes.

But if he wins, The Wave will be official, ratified by actual voters. As in the summer of 2003 but more so, because so many more people will be paying attention, he will be the talk of the nation. His picture will be on every front page. He will be on, or be the subject of, the Sunday TV talk shows. His popularity will be the subject of political analysis, pop sociology, talk-show derision and academic blather. It will be heady stuff, and one of the challenges he will face is not to let it go to his head.

But his foes will really be out to get him, and they will have coalesced behind a single alternative. In the autumn of 2003, the conventional wisdom held that Clark would be that alternative. But it will depend on who has finished where in Iowa and New Hampshire, or which candidate has "exceeded expectations" in the first two contests.

Howard Dean and wife, Judith Steinberg, cheer the moment as Dean announces his candidacy for president in Burlington on June 23, 2003. (Rutland Herald *Photo by Vyto Starinskas*)

The conventional wisdom, based on what has happened in the past, is that the establishment will succeed. Insurgent candidates such as McCain in 2000 and Hart in 1984 eventually ran up against the obstacle of having to run in several states at once without enough money, enough organization, enough support from powerful office-holders and interest groups. This could happen to Dean.

But the conditions are not the same. Those earlier insurgents were up against dominant front-runners George W. Bush and Walter Mondale. There is no such front-runner in the 2003 Democratic race, no one who, in Kamarck's words, "can get beat early and still come back," as Mondale and Bush did after losing New Hampshire. Some Democrats were hoping Gen. Clark could fill that slot. Maybe; maybe not.

Besides, just because no insurgent has ever ridden The Wave to victory does not mean that this one won't. Hart came close in 1984. After stunning Mondale in New Hampshire, he won the primaries in Florida and even in Alabama, where he had no campaign organization to speak of. Had Mondale not narrowly won Georgia that same day, Hart might well have been nominated.

"I could teach this one flat as well as round," says Mark Siegel. "Because he will be riding The Wave, and because of the Internet, he will have money. This kind of capability makes an insurgency possible. If you're well-funded, if you have the money up front, you can swamp the party."

Elaine Kamarck agrees. "The big difference is the Internet. Before, you couldn't turn The Wave into cash. Now you can do it instantaneously. If he wins New Hampshire, he'll be able to raise 19 to 20 million dollars a week."

If he does not swamp the party early, Dean could hit a rough patch. The states that vote a week after New Hampshire — Delaware, Missouri, Oklahoma, Arizona, New Mexico and North Dakota — do not appear to be the most Dean-friendly parts of the country. Whether his Wave will be strong enough to ride over these shoals is one of those imponderables over which political observers spend hours seeking answers, but rarely finding them. And, of course, what no one can predict is whether Dean will beat himself — which he is totally capable of doing.

For example, he can be prickly. When someone calling into a radio show criticized him for signing the civil unions bill in private, Dean shot back that the question was "The silliest thing I ever heard," and later told reporters that the question was obviously "a plant" by his political foes. But there was no way he could be sure of that. At campaign appearances, he sometimes argues with voters instead of talking to them. If he lets his petulance show at the wrong time — on national TV — and against the wrong person — a nice older woman voter who asks him a simple question — he could hurt himself.

In early autumn, Dean found himself caught in a political pincer — still being reviled as too liberal by some, but now attacked for being too conservative by Gephardt and Kerry, who brought up Dean's mid-1990s support for cutting the Medicare budget.

"You've been saying for many months that you're the head of the Democratic wing of the Democratic Party," Gephardt said in a late-September debate. "I think you're just winging it."

"That is flat-out false," Dean shot back, a bit testily in the view of some commentators, but perhaps appropriately tough to the average voter.

These attacks from the left test Dean's political agility. He had already figured out how to blunt the "too liberal" attack — by bringing up the "Birkenstock" image himself, by telling audiences he will "be a little bit like" John McCain, by saying he can't be such a liberal because "I'm not a big gun-control guy."

Even his liberal positions, he makes clear, are more moderate than radical. "I do not believe in free health care or free anything," he says. "If you want to totally reform the health care system, I'm not your guy. Just expand the system we already have to include everybody. I'm not interested in having an argument about what the best health care system is."

Having figured out how to portray himself as a pragmatic moderate, not a wacky lefty, Dean now has to figure out how to maintain his credentials as a "real Democrat." If he can do that, and portray himself as tough, not nasty, he could get nominated.

And elected? Americans tend to re-elect their presidents absent convincing reasons not to. The most powerful of those reasons are a shaky economy at home and messy entanglements abroad. Both prevail toward the end of 2003, which explains why George W. Bush is political Superman no longer. Even if the economy picks up, Bush is likely to be the first president since Herbert Hoover to preside over a nation with fewer jobs at the end of his term than at its beginning. Hoover was not re-elected.

As the election year approaches, the electorate appears split into almost even thirds. At least a third of the voters like and agree with George W. Bush. Another third opposes him. In Bush's favor, most of the third third seems to like him as a person and trust him as a leader. In the Democrats' favor, most of that same third group also disagrees with Bush on most issues.

If he is the Democratic nominee, Dean is likely to ask Ronald Reagan's famous question of 1980: Are you better off than you were four years ago? It will be interesting to see how Middle America answers that question.

But Dean would have his own questions to answer. No doubt Republican strategists have videotapes of Dean saying "I suppose that's a good thing" about the ouster of Saddam Hussein. Not to mention videotape of one of his Democratic opponents claiming Dean's tax proposal could cost some "middle-class families" $2,000 a year. Both tapes can be expected on Bush campaign commercials.

The "I suppose" line might not be as effective as Republicans hoped in April 2003 when the Iraq war seemed an unqualified success. The tax issue can be more trouble for Dean even if his opponents have bizarrely re-defined "middle class" to mean anyone making less than $200,000 a year. Dean's response — that the real middle class saved nothing because "their college tuitions went up, their property taxes went up, fire and police and first response services are going down" — is not without substance, but it is a difficult sell among a tax-averse electorate dominated by a sound-bite political culture.

Republicans may not produce commercials about Vermont's civil unions law, instead keeping it in the public mind by supporting a constitutional amendment defining marriage. Dean's response here is that he did what he thought was right regardless of the political damage.

"I never got a chance to ask myself whether signing it was a good idea or not," he says, "because I knew that if I were willing to sell out the rights of a whole group of human beings because it might be politically inconvenient for a future office I might run for, then I had wasted my time in public service."

The message to middle-of-the-road voters is clear: You

might disagree with me on this issue, but I am a man of principle. Gay rights has never before been an issue in a national election campaign, so no one can predict its salience.

Still, the conventional wisdom holds that if Dean should be the nominee, Bush would beat him. Then again, the conventional wisdom not long ago was that Dean had no chance to be nominated. He's ahead of the conventional wisdom one-to-zip, and was still the front-runner after Clark entered the race.

Besides, events influence elections more than do political strategies. Anything can happen in the next year — another terrorist attack, success or failure of the occupation in Iraq, economic growth or a "double-dip" recession. Depending on how they work out, in a few years Americans may be calling Howard Dean that doctor from Vermont who made such a splash for a few months before fading back to the relative obscurity of his medical practice, a university presidency, or the stewardship of a prestigious foundation.

Then again, they might be calling him Mr. President.

Jon Margolis

Howard Dean, second from right, poses
with his brothers, from left,
Charlie, Jim and Bill.
(AP Photo/Files)

CHAPTER 2

Years That Shaped Him

Under a beige tent on a steamy late-summer evening in Middletown, Rhode Island, Howard Dean once again stood before a microphone, a crowd gathered 'round to take his measure. August 2003 had been a heady — and somewhat frenetic — month for the Democratic presidential front-runner, with campaign stops across the country far from his home state of Vermont. But here, under this tent in this bucolic corner of Rhode Island, Dean was on turf as familiar as any in Vermont — and among people who knew him long before pollsters began charting his mass appeal.

For directly across the street was the campus of St. George's School, an Episcopalian bastion of 19th-century red brick and neo-Gothic towers, where Dean was a boarding student from age 13 until his graduation in 1966. Now, 37 years later, Dean was standing before a linen-jacketed group of prominent Democrats, as he has at so many campaign stops. But here the connection was personal.

The crowd included Rhode Island's legendary patrician senator, Claiborne Pell, who retired from the Senate after six terms and now gets around in a wheelchair. Pell was accompanied by his son Toby, Dean's classmate at St. George's, and Toby was accompanied by his wife and daughter. Indeed, the tent was filled with many well-wishers — many of no particular party affiliation — who had paid as much as $1,000 to hear the man they'd known in prep school. Chris Corkery, Dean's football coach, was there, as was Hays Rockwell, the former Episcopal bishop of St. Louis whose first posting out of the seminary had been to St. George's, and who had taught 16-year-old Howard philosophy.

It was a singular moment for Dean as he looked out at faces from a time when neither he nor anyone else present could have imagined this St. George's boy as candidate for president of the United States. The path that would take him from St. George's onto the national political stage was meandering, to say the least. Yet, the roots of his candidacy and manner in which Dean presents himself to voters, longtime acquaintances say, are resonant of the Howard they knew in school.

SHELTERED WORLD

St. George's in Dean's day was a sheltered world of old money and family ties. Many of the boys attended because their fathers and grandfathers had. "My father went there, my brother went there, my son went there and all of the Dean brothers went there," says Toby Pell, who actually was in the minority as a boy with local ties. While the school's spectacularly lush campus, on a bluff overlooking the Atlantic Ocean, is in Rhode Island, most of Dean's classmates came from well-to-do families in New York, Philadelphia and Boston. No minority students were at St. George's when Dean enrolled, though the school's Web site today boasts "24 percent students of color." Quips Lucien Wulsin Jr., who attended with his younger brother, Harry, during the 1960s: "The Wulsins were the diversity. We were Catholics from Cincinnati."

Howard Dean was part of the New York contingent. The son, grandson and great-grandson of Wall Street stock and bond brokers, he'd grown up on Manhattan's Park Avenue and at the family's second home in East Hampton at the tip of Long Island, where his parents were members of the exclusive Maidstone Club. As a youngster, he attended the Browning School, a private boys school on East 62nd Street. But from ninth grade on, Dean was at St. George's. After graduation, he spent an exchange year at an English boarding school, went on to major in political science at Yale University — President Bush's alma mater — then attended medical school.

That Bush and Dean graduated from the same Ivy League university, together with the parallel of their silver-spoon childhoods, has been much noted in the press — a comparison that irks Dean supporters, particularly those who were his schoolmates. John Allen, a Greenwich, Connecticut–based management consultant and Dean's roommate at St. George's, is one. Allen scoffs at the preppie stereotype that began to dog Dean when he stepped out of the insular environment of Vermont into the national political arena. "He did grow up on Park Avenue; he did go to all these schools, but that doesn't mean he's a snob," Allen contends.

Interviews with other schoolmates of Dean — at St. George's, Yale and, later, Albert Einstein College of Medicine — lend support. Indeed, their descriptions of the boy, the college student and the young man intent on a medical career are remarkably consistent. Howard Dean, according to these classmates, stood out for his sincerity, for a serious turn of mind, and for an almost ferocious tenacity in pursuing his goals. Given his family lineage, they contend,

> "We were always playing sports, whether it was ice hockey or softball or swimming or sailing. The whole thing was outdoors."
>
> *Howard Dean, 2003 Interview*

Dean could have coasted into a career on Wall Street and a life of WASP social prominence. Instead, after working briefly at a brokerage house, he rejected Wall Street and went to medical school, married outside his religion, moved to Vermont and sent his children to public school despite having the financial means to replicate the privilege of his own education. Finally, he entered the political ring, where pedigree is no protection against the hard knocks of a presidential contest.

The candidate's sometimes rough-edged public demeanor also doesn't surprise his old classmates. From early school days, these acquaintances say, Dean demonstrated strong convictions and an action-oriented approach to problem solving. He was blunt-spoken then as now, a characteristic that was part of his appeal as a friend and classmate, however alarming it may be to political strategists now charged with polishing Dean for prime time.

ST. GEORGE'S YEARS

Howard Brush Dean III was born on November 17, 1948, the first of four sons of Howard B. Dean Jr., a stock broker, and Andrée Maitland Dean, an art and antiques appraiser. His brother Charles was born 15 months later, then came James, followed by William. Raised to be independent and self-reliant, the brothers were nevertheless close; Dean's surviving brothers, Jim and Bill, today are active in his campaign.

Howard Dean speaks fondly of a childhood primarily centered on the family's summer and weekend home in East Hampton, a seaside community now crowded with oceanfront mansions but more rural and relaxed when Dean was a child.

"We were always playing sports, whether it was ice hockey or softball or swimming or sailing," Dean recalls. "The whole thing was outdoors." That preoccupation with sports made the transition to boarding school fairly seamless, says Dean, since life at St. George's revolved almost as much around athletics as academics.

Dean's father pursued the family line of work on Wall Street, following in the footsteps of his father and grandfather. But Dean family members, also irked by the stereotype of indolent affluence, assert that all had to make their fortunes as workers and ultimately partners in brokerage firms, not inheritors. It is a source of amusement for the family that as Howard Dean comes under public scrutiny and the outline of his personal history becomes known, the candidate is presumed to be a descendant of a founder of the old Dean Witter brokerage house.

"That's so foolish," laughs Dean's mother, Andrée. "Because, you know, Dean Witter was one person, a man called Dean Witter."

By all accounts, Dean's late father was a formidable presence, both revered and, at times, feared by his sons. Charming and witty, "Big Howard," as Andrée Dean dubs him in interviews to avoid confusion with her son, also was hard driving, politically conservative and fiscally tight. Family wealth notwithstanding, his sons had to earn their spending money, usually through household chores. Andrée Dean recalls that her husband cajoled even the boys' friends into raking leaves or trimming trees at the country house, then rewarded them with only a fraction of what other dads were paying.

Howard Dean, right, was a multi-sport athlete at St. George's prep school in Middletown, Rhode Island.
(Courtesy St. George's School)

At home, adds Jim Dean, "Pops was a bit of a micro-manager." When the boys came home on school vacations, whether from prep school or college, the conversations might start casually enough. But they quickly became grillings. The elder Dean loathed half-baked political theories and stratagems that lacked practical fallback plans should things go awry.

"He'd ask you what you were doing," Jim Dean recalls, "and then when you told him, he'd bore in and demand: 'How are you going to accomplish that?' and 'What are you going to do if that doesn't work?'"

Young Howard held his own with Big Howard, though there was often heat in the exchange, especially during the Yale years, when the younger Dean, influenced by campus unrest over civil rights and the Vietnam War, aired ever-more-liberal political views on his visits home.

"He'd make these declarations that were a bit much," says Mrs. Dean, recalling battles between the Howards. "But he would express them, no matter what."

Unlike the Pell family, the Deans did not have ties to St. George's School when they selected it for their sons. Big Howard had gone to Pomfret, a rival boarding school in Connecticut that, like St. George's, was in the second tier of academic prep schools, overshadowed by Ivy League feeder schools such as St. Paul's and Exeter. Young Howard "was always pretty smart in school," says his mother, but she and her husband were looking for more than academics. They wanted an environment where their sons would be happy away from home, and where moral and personal standards of conduct would be upheld. Big Howard's alma mater failed that litmus test on an inspection tour in 1961.

> As an upperclassman, Howard Dean was elected prefect, a position of honor and responsibility reserved for boys who could command the respect of their peers as well as faculty.

"We went to the chapel on Sunday and the students were so rude, they talked all through the service, and they didn't stand up to sing or anything," Mrs. Dean recalls of their visit to Pomfret. At St. George's, the Deans found masters (teachers) who were approachable and who truly seemed to enjoy teaching teenage boys, Mrs. Dean says.

She says the family sent the boys away to school to set them on the road to independence. Howard Dean says his years at St. George's did that and more for him.

"From an early age, we had to make decisions that had to do

with right and wrong without parental guidance," says Dean, adding that living in a community of adolescent boys of varying abilities and personalities also forced one to learn "the limits of your own selfishness."

"In adolescence, you tend toward being a selfish person," explains Dean, whose children are teenagers. "It is a narcissistic, self-absorbed period in your life. And when you are living in a very communal environment, like a boarding school, you can't do that." You have to find a way to fit in, Dean says, and also to help those having a harder time. "You come to be appreciative of other people's feeling in a way that you might not be when you are at home fighting your parents all the time."

Dean says he also valued the close relationships with teachers at St. George's, who might push hard in class, but substituted for parents when the need arose. He mentions a history teacher, William Schenck, who is retired now but nevertheless showed up at one of the Rhode Island fund-raisers to pepper his former student with questions about Middle East policy.

"He was one of those people you went and talked to when things weren't going well in your life," Dean says and then laughs, recalling a different Mr. Schenck in the classroom. "He scared the hell out of us. . . . He was exacting and he did not like fuzzy thinking." If a student was unprepared, the consequences were mortifying: "I can remember to this day. . . . He'd say to you: 'You don't know, young Dean, do you? You don't know, and why, pray tell, don't you know?'"

At St. George's, classmates and teachers say Dean was popular and respected, neither prissy nor wild. "He was very earnest, someone you could count on," recalls Denis O'Neill, a St. George's classmate, now a film producer in Beverly Hills, California. "What you saw was just who he was."

Harry Wulsin, Lucien's younger brother and Dean's classmate, says Dean could also be brutally direct. Among his friends, it was a trait that engendered respect, if you weren't intimidated. "Whatever his opinions were, he was very strong," says Wulsin, a Florida businessman. "You were either with him or against him, but he wasn't strident or demeaning if you didn't agree. He would never say in an argument, 'You're stupid to think that way.'"

Dean's prep school teachers remember him as bright and serious about his studies, though not at the top of the class. A determined rather than a natural athlete, he played football and was co-captain of the wrestling team. Coaches delighted in his competitive drive, work ethic and focus. Football coach Corkery remembers the boy's astonishing success at right guard. "For a little guy — he wasn't much bigger than he is now — he was surprisingly effective against much bigger kids," Corkery recalls. "He was explosive, and I think it also surprised them that he hit with such velocity." To beef up his 5-foot-8 frame, Dean lifted weights, keeping a set of barbells in his dorm room. That wasn't something high school kids did in the '60s to the extent they do today. Says Harry Wulsin, "We nicknamed him Sgt. Rock," after the muscle-bound comic book hero.

As an upperclassman, Dean was elected prefect, a position of honor and responsibility reserved for boys who could command the respect of their peers as well as faculty. Prefects were school leaders who also acted as dorm supervisors of younger boys, enforcing rules on bedtime and bed-making, but also helping youngsters who were homesick or struggling with schoolwork. The Rev. Rockwell and his wife were house fellows in Auchincloss, where Dean was second-floor prefect. "We could go out for the evening and be confident that everything would be under control with Howard in charge," Mr. Rockwell recalls.

Two classes below Howard was his brother, Charlie. Those asked to recollect the candidate as a youth often mention Charlie by way of contrast. The younger brother, they say, was fun-loving and charming — a natural politician, though an indifferent student. Howard was less glib, more intense. While Howard excelled at sports and academics, Charlie worked the crowd. By his senior year, Charlie was president of the St. George's student body. Later, he rose to student government leader at the University of North Carolina at Chapel Hill.

Richard Dulaney, who knew both brothers growing up, says he's teased Howard Dean in recent months, saying that if Charlie were alive, he'd be the one running for president.

Charlie Dean was killed while traveling in Southeast Asia in 1974. Some speculate that his brother's death changed the direction of Howard Dean's life, propelling him into a political world he might not otherwise have entered. But most of Howard's old friends say Dean was already headed in the direction of public service of some kind, shaped as so many of his generation were by the tumult of the times, as well as by his own need to do something rather than just talk about issues that were important to him. This was evident during the Yale years, when Dean, inspired by the civil rights movement, requested black roommates during his freshman year and later became involved in a mentoring program for disadvantaged minority children in New Haven.

At St. George's, however, the early stirrings of racial protest were muted by the school's determined isolation amid 200 acres of gardens and playing fields. Since its founding in 1896 to prepare boys for lives of "constructive service to the world and to God," St. George's had secured its place by hewing to tradition and resisting the impulse to embrace social trends deemed fleeting. Student life was organized accordingly.

Boys in the ninth grade were allowed only one overnight per semester, and one full weekend home per year. Trips to nearby Newport (in Dean's time a Navy port teeming with sailors, unlike the posh resort it is today) were limited to one per month, for which students had to sign up, sign out and sign back in. The school day ran from 8:30 a.m. to 2:30 p.m., after which came mandatory sports until 5:30 p.m., showers, chapel, dinner, study hall and lights out at 10 p.m. Saturdays featured chapel again, classes until noon, then sports competitions with other schools, followed perhaps by a dance with a nearby girls school. On Sundays, there were two chapel sessions. "It was run like a military base," says Toby Pell. "Everything was geared to the 'hilltop.' . . . Interaction with the town was not encouraged."

But the turmoil of the '60s could not be entirely shut out,

and St. George's would change radically during Howard Dean's years and immediately afterward. A sophomore class straw poll preceding the 1960 presidential election yielded only two votes for Democrat John F. Kennedy, the remaining 50-odd going to Republican Richard Nixon. The results said much about the families who sent their sons to St. George's, but it also signified the end of an era. Kennedy would win the election, the youngest elected president in history, and a Catholic, too. In Dean's first year, federal marshals were escorting James Meredith into the University of Mississippi to enforce court-ordered racial integration. In his second year, the president who'd ordered the marshals to Mississippi was assassinated, an event no less horrifying on the "hilltop" than in the rest of the nation.

"You have to understand that the moral question for people in the '60s, for students and their teachers, was integration," says the Rev. Rockwell. He preached on civil rights, and he and other activist faculty aired their views in the classroom, challenging

> "He shows up and first of all, his hair is kind of long, he's wearing these mod clothes and, well, he didn't know or care too much about Vietnam when he left, but he sure did when he came back."
>
> *Jim Dean,*
> *Brother*

students to delve into issues of social inequity. Simultaneously, faculty members were pushing the school to act on its moral precepts. The specific question of whether St. George's could remain all-white sparked battles within the faculty and board of trustees. In the end, the school decided to integrate, and the class after Howard Dean's was selected to receive the first black students.

Three poor Newport boys were offered scholarships, but only one — a bright and personable youth, who was also a good athlete — accepted. These attributes were ingredients for success at St. George's, but the story did not have a happy ending.

To this day, according to Mr. Rockwell, what happened to the teenager haunts those who were his teachers and classmates. Arrested during a summer break from school for beating his foster mother and setting fire to their home, the boy would serve time in prison and die, a suicide, at age 19.

During this time of ferment, in the summer of 1965, Howard Dean made his first foray out of the cocoon of his upbringing. He traveled to Florida with two friends for a job on a cattle ranch. There, he found himself in an almost entirely Spanish-speaking environment, his school French useless. "Nobody spoke English except the ranch manager," recalls Dean. (His children, the candidate notes, are studying "practical" languages, namely Spanish and Chinese.)

A YEAR'S WAIT

Dean graduated from St. George's in 1966 and was accepted by Yale, where his father and grandfather had gone. It was cause for celebration in the Dean household, but young Howard deferred his acceptance for a year. Dean says he did so partly because he wanted to spend time abroad and partly because his father thought he was too young for college.

That assessment, Dean says, reflected the elder Dean's own hard-earned perspective on the maturity required for success. Like young Howard, Big Howard was 17 when he graduated from prep school. He went directly to Yale, where his sons say he whooped it up for two years until the university kicked him out. He had failed a key course — and also, apparently, failed to get the message, because he flunked the same course sophomore year.

"My grandfather was pissed, you can imagine," says Bill Dean. But Big Howard — actually a diminutive man — was nothing if not determined. Stricken with diphtheria as a toddler, he had survived only because of a tracheostomy enabling him to breathe. The tracheostomy — a tube surgically inserted through the front of the throat into the windpipe — had kept the elder Howard from sports and many other activities of boyhood. Though he outgrew the need for it, the treatment left him with a distinctive raspy voice and a vulnerability to injury and infection. After leaving Yale, he wanted to go overseas where World War II was under way, but the military rejected him on medical grounds. He got there anyway, Howard Dean says admiringly, via a civilian job providing logistical support to Allied supply lines in North Africa. "My father lived an incredible existence," says Dean. "He had to work really hard to overcome all his disabilities." Big Howard kept pushing, living in India for a year, and then China, where he lent his supply line savvy to the Chinese National Air Corps in the fight against the Japanese.

Howard and Jim Dean say their father loved the adventure of these overseas years, because they broadened the reach of his own sheltered upbringing. He sampled diverse cultures, people and political views, and learned to speak several languages. He returned home when his father became ill, according to Howard Dean, and stayed to shoulder the responsibilities of family and livelihood. But he retained the friendships made abroad and, by example, instilled in his older sons the importance of travel and worldly perspective. So it was that Howard Dean came to spend a year at Felsted, an English boarding school, before attending Yale.

At Felsted, Dean befriended a Nigerian boy and traveled to Africa to visit his family. He also took advantage of school vacations to travel extensively, including Eastern Europe in order to witness life behind the Iron Curtain. This was unusual for American and Western European travelers in the '60s, amid Cold War tensions. On one vacation, Dean says, he and seven school friends piled into a Land Rover and drove to Turkey via Bulgaria and the former Yugoslavia. Wherever they stayed, one boy would sleep on the floor by the door of the room to guard against intruders. "We thought it was dangerous, but it turned out not to be," Dean says.

By his own account and those of family members, Dean returned from England greatly changed from the blue-blazered preppie of the previous year. "This Europe trip was a real eye-opener for Howard," Jim Dean says, noting some external changes that raised eyebrows at home. "He shows up and first of all, his hair is kind of long, he's wearing these mod clothes and, well, he didn't know or care too much about Vietnam when he left, but he sure did when he came back."

Howard Dean says Felsted — and the summer on the ranch in Florida — led him to think more broadly about diversity. The year in England presented other challenges, too. As a lone American among English and international students, Dean says, he was repeatedly asked to explain the racial strife at home and U.S. policies in Vietnam. He had to stretch to hold his own, and he wanted to keep stretching. "I think I intrinsically recognized that I'd had a sheltered upbringing, and I was tired of it," he says. When Yale sent him a housing questionnaire to learn his roommate preferences (Neatnik? Smoker? Night owl?), Dean answered that he wanted a black roommate.

Life at Yale

Yale responded by assigning him to a four-person suite with two black students from the South and an Italian-American from small-town Pennsylvania who came to the school to play football. They lived in Wright Hall, one of the oldest buildings at Yale.

That first year "was the most important in terms of what I learned," says Dean, crediting those with whom he lived, all of whom he still counts as friends. But the friendships with his black roommates did not happen overnight.

"It was the height of the civil rights movement, and there was enormous tension because they didn't know any white people and I didn't know any black people and we had a hell of a lot of learning to do," Dean remembers. Just finding the right words in conversation so as not to give offense was a challenge.

One black roommate, Ralph Dawson, now a Manhattan lawyer, says of Dean during the Yale years:

"I would say he was different from most people in that he was not a lock-step thinker. Most people, especially to some extent back then when we were all trying to develop our view of the world, tended to take kind of a dialectical approach to things. That was not Howard. I think you see some of that even today. . . . He doesn't say, 'Because I believe in one, two and three, therefore I must believe in four and five.' He reserves the right to examine the process along the way."

On race and on Vietnam, Dawson says, Dean was committed but determinedly non-violent. His hero was Martin Luther King Jr., not Stokely Carmichael. Dawson, on the other hand, found King's turn-the-other-cheek philosophy too limiting and says he wound up getting arrested in a demonstration outside City Hall in New Haven after a shoving match with a plainclothes police officer.

"Howard would be more inclined to look at the problem, take like a piece of it, and try to accomplish what he could accomplish," Dawson says, noting Dean's volunteer work in New Haven ghettos as teacher and mentor to needy minority youngsters. One of those children was a youngster named Karl.

"Howard would take this kid Karl around with him," recalls former classmate Richard Dulaney. "Karl would come over to the campus and sit in the dining hall and have lunch with us or you'd walk into Howard's room and there's Karl. . . . I don't want to over-paint the time he spent with him in terms of hours, but what was notable was that the rest of us could not have cared less. It wasn't something we would have gone and done."

In April 1968, still their freshman year, King was assassinated; in June, Robert F. Kennedy, the Democratic presidential hopeful, was gunned down. Their deaths punctuated a transformative year for Dean and his classmates. Dean says those historic events solidified in his mind the importance of tolerance and understanding diverse points of view.

> "Howard would be more inclined to look at the problem, take like a piece of it, and try to accomplish what he could accomplish."
>
> *Ralph Dawson,*
> *Former Roommate*

Largely for that reason, Dean says, he and his wife, Judith

Steinberg, decided to send their children to public schools in Burlington, Vermont's largest city, where he lives.

"It is a values-based choice," explains Dean of public education. "I value diversity and I value the understanding that I found hard to come by. I found it as a freshman in college; I found it when I did this work [on the Florida ranch] and I found it when I went to England and lived and traveled all over Europe and North Africa."

Dean's definition of diversity goes beyond race. He notes that Burlington in recent years has become home to several refugee groups; the high school's signs feature Bosnian and Vietnamese in addition to English. And although Vermont's population is far whiter than most states, income and cultural backgrounds range widely.

DISTRACTIONS AT YALE

Dean's academic record at Yale was unimpressive. His mother says she saw few grades above average, and the serious, focused student of prep school days vanishes from descriptions by Yale contemporaries. Classmates say they remember greater dedication on Dean's part to intramural sports, parties and late-night bridge games than to his studies.

"I remember endless, endless hours of playing bridge," recalls David Berg, a New Haven psychologist who was at Yale with Dean. "Howard played bridge for the socialness of it — the four people playing, the two or three people watching — the drama of succeeding and failing at the bridge table and the histrionics that ensued." Berg adds that Dean was naturally charismatic, a "life-of-the party sort of person without really trying."

"There are some people who have to be the center of attention, but with Howard you never felt like he had to be the center of attention and yet most of the time, in most rooms he was in, or at most parties he was at, he was," explains Berg. "I don't know exactly how to convey this, but there are people who try and who have cultivated this sort of being this center of attention and then there are people who just are. Howard was the latter in the sense that people liked being around him. He would be funny; he would be outrageous; he would be self-deprecatory — there was some sort of combination that made him somebody who folks just liked to be around and have around. He wasn't terribly studious in the first two or three years . . . that's probably an understatement . . . and yet he was one of the few people who read the *New York Times* every day."

Dean acknowledges that his classwork got short shrift, though he partly blames the era. With all the political turmoil, no one in his circle of friends was terribly focused on grades or job prospects after graduation. He contrasts his experience with that of his younger brother Bill, who attended the University of Vermont five years later when the U.S. economy was in recession. Dean recalls visiting Bill and expecting an atmosphere similar to what he experienced at Yale. Instead, he found the library jammed with students hunched over their books. Dean says he and Bill talked about the differences. "I said, 'We just lived from day to day.' And he said, 'What could you guys have been thinking?'"

Dean at Yale also liked his beer, enough that it became an issue leading to his decision to abstain from alcohol entirely, shortly after he and Steinberg married in 1981. Dean once told *New York Magazine* that he didn't handle liquor well. "I tended to misbehave. I had a hangover the next day," he is quoted as saying, adding: "What's funny when you're 18 isn't funny when you're 30, so I just quit."

If his academic performance was less than exemplary, Dean at college showed consistency in the character trait observed at St. George's: a plainspoken, action-oriented approach to what he believes, where others might give only lip service. Friendship was no protection from Dean broadsides, if he thought someone was in the wrong.

Richard Willing, a national correspondent for *USA Today,* remembers an incident during one of the dorm touch football games in which Dean lit into him for roughing up a player neither of them particularly liked. Willing says he and Dean met on the first day of school. "He was the first person I met at Yale.

He helped me and my father carry my footlocker to my room, which adjoined his room." Willing and Dean also overcame differences in background to cement their friendship. A product of Irish immigrants and public school, Willing was attending Yale on an ROTC scholarship. Dean, after his year in England, arrived with anti–Vietnam War sentiments already full-blown. Their differences on this issue would occasion many debates, but no hard feelings until the football game.

> "He would be funny; he would be outrageous; he would be self-deprecatory — there was some sort of combination that made him somebody who folks just liked to be around and have around."
>
> *David Berg,*
> *Psychologist/Classmate*

The game consisted of a core group of dormitory friends, but on this day they had let in the teenage son of the Rev. William Sloane Coffin, Yale's radical anti-war chaplain. Dean saw Willing throw what he considered an unnecessarily hard block at the boy, knocking him down. Willing acknowledges that he might have hit Coffin's son too aggressively but adds that the college students generally considered him a nuisance. Nevertheless, he remembers Dean "jumping on me right away," having seen more in Willing's action than energetic play.

"He yelled 'Willing!' right there on the field, and then said, 'You're just mad because of his father. . . . Knock it off!' I defended myself, saying the kid ran into me or something like that, but he said, 'Aw, don't give me that garbage.' I'm pretty sure the game ended right there."

Willing recalls the incident as an example of the line Dean drew between personal and intellectual disagreements — which he readily accepted — and conduct. His views on right and wrong regarding the latter "were not shakable at any level," says Willing.

GRADUATION DAY

The commencement for Dean's class in the spring of 1971 epitomized the social and political turmoil that engulfed college campuses of that era. Most of the class had arrived from prep schools, sporting crew cuts and Bass Weejuns. There were no women at Yale then, and jackets and ties were required in the dining halls. By graduation, the dress code was gone, Yale was co-ed and the admissions policy had tilted in favor of public school applicants. Jim Dean laughs at the memory of Howard's graduation, when the younger Dean boys and parents arrived dressed up for what Big Howard considered a milestone family event.

"The scene was just unbelievable," says Jim, who describes himself at the time as a sullen 17-year-old who was ordered with his brothers to wear suits for the occasion. "One service union was on strike; [West German] Chancellor Willie Brandt was the speaker, and there was a huge protest going on. We get to Howard's room and he isn't there, but there are a bunch of people apparently living there who aren't Yale students but are kind of street people with tattoos and all. Dad was cordial, but his voice was pretty low and gravelly and we knew he wasn't too happy. Then we get to the graduation ceremony and here are all these people in sandals and shorts and bare legs sticking out from under their graduation robes.

Howard Dean, second from right, was a lineman on his college's intramural football team at Yale in 1970.
(Courtesy of Richard Willing)

"Dad was just getting redder and redder, and all of a sudden my brother Billy leans over and elbows him and says, 'Hey, Dad, here you are at your first Yale graduation.'" It was a joking reference to the fact that Big Howard had never graduated, but the older brothers froze, expecting an explosion of temper. Instead, their father burst out laughing. The collision between one generation's expectations and the next one's reality could not have been more vividly sketched, and Big Howard yielded to the inevitable.

Dean emerged from Yale with the Vietnam War still raging. But he says that a back problem, spondylolisthesis, which is caused by misaligned vertebrae in the lower back, resulted in a medical deferment. He received a 1-Y classification from his draft board, which still would have made him available for service in the event of a national emergency. With no clear idea of what he wanted to do, Dean went off to Colorado to ski, supporting himself with a dishwashing job in Aspen. A year later, he returned home to earn a living. It seemed logical that Howard Dean III would follow family tradition to Wall Street.

"Big Howard fixed it up, and he went down and took an exam that tells you if you are any good at this or not, and he got very high marks," recalls Andrée Dean. "Actually, he did very well in his job, but I guess he wasn't very happy and decided to go to medical school instead."

A CAREER DECISION

Howard Dean did not decide overnight to become a doctor. He carefully tested not only his inclination, but his aptitude for something so out of step with Dean family tradition. While continuing to work as a stockbroker, he quietly began taking night courses at Columbia University in biology, organic chemistry and other prerequisites for medical school. He also volunteered at a Manhattan hospital to see if working with sick people was his thing.

Exactly when Dean's interest in a medical career took hold is unclear, even to those close to him. Longtime acquaintances say Dean was never one to turn decisions over to a majority vote, nor was he inclined to confide personal leanings before undertaking his own analysis.

Dean has said in published reports that even as a Yale student, he had thought about being a doctor or teaching because they were professions that enabled one to "change the world in some way." Yet he took no pre-med courses, and Yale friends say that if Dean was considering medicine, he never let on. "I knew the guy for four years, and I don't think he came within smelling distance of a science course," says David Berg, who today teaches at Yale University School of Medicine. Berg believes Dean began to seriously consider medicine only after becoming disillusioned with Wall Street. Like so many young people in their first years out of college, Dean found his direction by discovering what he didn't like. Berg's first inkling came during a post-college visit when Dean was already working on Wall Street and living in an apartment in Manhattan's West Village. Berg, a graduate student at the University of Michigan, would stay with Dean when he came to New York to do research.

"One time I'm there and he says, 'I'm thinking about taking pre-med courses and going to med school,'" recalls Berg. ". . . And my jaw dropped. I said, 'What is this about? This is unbelievable!' I mean, I knew he wanted to get out of stock brokering because it's mostly sales, and he's just not a salesperson, in the sense of convincing somebody to buy something that they don't want, so I knew he wasn't long for that. But medicine was a shock.

"He said he would like to do something — I think his words were — 'morally unimpeachable,'" Berg recalls. "That is, something that's a good that everybody can agree makes a contribution to the general welfare."

> Howard Dean shies away from the subject of Charlie's death in interviews but has ' acknowledged suffering from "survivor's guilt and anger."

Dean didn't tell his parents until he had decided to register for pre-med courses at Columbia. Andrée Dean, who earned her undergraduate degree from Columbia when her children were away at school, says she found out accidentally, when she ran into her son on campus.

"Many of us — mothers mostly, women with household responsibilities — who went to college later in life belonged to an organization called Friends of General Studies, and we volunteered at the registration tables, helping women, older students like ourselves, to know what was a reasonable course load," Mrs. Dean recalls. "I was sitting there one day and all of a sudden I heard a familiar voice saying, 'Do you have chemistry at night?' Well, I looked up and there was Howard, and he saw me and we were both very surprised. That was the first I heard about his interest in medical school. The cat was out of the bag!"

She speculates that her son decided on his own because he didn't want to upset his father until he was absolutely sure. When that moment came, he stuck to his guns, much as he had during dinner table debates years before. Dean has been quoted as saying that he took his father out, "fed him three martinis," and told him he was leaving Wall Street.

FAMILY TRAGEDY

Dean continued to work on Wall Street while completing two years of pre-medical coursework at Columbia. During this time tragedy struck the family, leaving Howard Dean, his parents and brothers with a sorrow that lingers three decades later.

Like his father and older brother, Charlie Dean had set off on a foreign adventure, but in a different frame of mind. According to Jim Dean, he left deeply disillusioned by the outcome of the presidential election of 1972.

Charlie was the most ideological of the brothers; Jim Dean contrasts Charlie's political activism with Howard's "more pragmatic" approach to politics as a problem-solving tool (Jim Dean now works full time for the Dean for America campaign.). Charlie's interest in politics also developed earlier in life. Even as a young teenager, Charlie "would go out on the streets and pass out leaflets" for candidates and causes, Jim Dean recalls. After graduating in 1972 from the University of North Carolina at Chapel Hill, Charlie stayed on to spearhead the local campaign of anti-war Democrat George McGovern. McGovern's loss in 49 of the 50 states came as a shock. "He decided to just go away for a while," according to Jim. "My uncle got him on a freighter to Japan."

Over the next several months, Charlie backpacked through Asia, finally arriving in Australia, where he stayed for six months with friends. Then he and an Australian took off for Southeast Asia. The trail there is harder to reconstruct. Some speculate — the Dean family doesn't buy it — that Charlie was doing intelligence work for the United States, based on the fact that after he disappeared, U.S. authorities classified him as a prisoner of war or missing in action. What the family does know is that Laotian rebels captured Charlie and his companion as they traveled by ferry on the Mekong River. They were held for three months, then executed. "We think that the North Vietnamese basically ordered them killed," Howard Dean said in a *Newsweek* interview.

> "He had an exceptional level of commitment and maturity, and he had a calming ability. Things did not bother him the way they did some of the rest of us."
>
> *Dr. Stephen Goldstone, Former Roommate*

Charlie's death — and the agony of his parents as they frantically sought to win their son's release — snapped Howard Dean into focus about his own life. He bore down on the premed courses as he'd never done at Yale, aced his exams and won acceptance to medical school. As for his own grief, Dean struggled privately. "It just wastes you," he told *New York Magazine.* "Everyone falls apart; they just fall apart in different ways." Dean's mother has expressed regret that the family was never able to come together to talk about their feelings because Big Howard got too upset. Later, the Deans and family friends endowed a scholarship at St. George's in Charlie's memory, intended, the citation reads, for students who have "demonstrated a concern for the community, the ability to lead and a sense of civic responsibility."

Dean shies away from the subject of Charlie's death in interviews but has acknowledged suffering from "survivor's guilt and anger." He misses his brother. They were close in age (Jim and Bill are, respectively, five and six years younger than Howard) and as small boys had shared a bedroom. Yet Dean has said he also resented the pain Charlie's death inflicted on the rest of the family and sought counseling in the 1980s to work through those feelings. Later, spurred by the emotional aftermath of the Sept. 11, 2001, terrorist attacks, Dean traveled to Laos to visit the spot where Charlie is believed to have been executed.

His death, friends say, had another effect: that of halting Dean's Yale-influenced drift into liberal politics. "It had a huge impact on Howard and moved him three or four notches to the right," asserts Richard Dulaney. He thinks it accounts for what he sees as Dean's "pragmatic" and "middle-of-the-road" approach to social and political issues.

Much of this is speculative, of course, calling into question the degree to which anyone can tease out the impact of a single event from other influential forces. Even Dean says he hasn't entirely worked it through. Nevertheless, there's no denying the seriousness of purpose that emerged in him during those difficult post-Yale years. The bright spot, after two years of grinding it out in night school, was his acceptance letter from Albert Einstein College of Medicine.

MEDICAL SCHOOL

Albert Einstein was not New York's premier medical school in the '70s, nor was it a likely place to find someone of Dean's background. But Dean had already traveled some distance from his WASP, preppie, Ivy League roots — and Einstein would take him farther.

The medical school's groundbreaking in 1953, under the auspices of Yeshiva University, a former Jewish theological seminary in the Bronx, was good news for those whose ambitions for a medical career had been stymied by social prejudices of the era. Simply put, Jews in the 1950s had a hard time getting into medical school, as did blacks, immigrants and women. Though it would open up opportunities for Jewish doctors,

Albert Einstein College of Medicine declared from the outset a non-discriminatory admissions policy. So even though Jews were in the majority, the first classes also had women and blacks, according to Stephen H. Lazar, the school's assistant director.

When Dean applied, Jews, minorities and women were well represented in U.S. medical schools. But prejudices of a different sort influenced admissions decisions. Older students who hadn't majored in the sciences as undergraduates were considered less desirable. Once again, Albert Einstein bucked the status quo, admitting students who had been in the workforce as well as foreign-born students, if their pre-med coursework and entrance examination scores met admissions standards, Lazar says. Howard Dean found a welcome at Albert Einstein.

Lazar, who worked in the student affairs office at the time, remembers Dean as "motivated and hard-working." Dean also stood out for his manners and social ease in the intense mix of sometimes one-dimensional medical students. "He was the kind of person who gives a big hello to the secretaries and means it," Lazar says. While at Einstein, Dean worked on the staff of a scientific journal, called the *Einstein Quarterly,* which offered a venue to students who wanted to publish their research or clinical insights. Dean also participated in Einstein's social medicine program, through which students were sent to work in poor neighborhoods of the city. The Bronx was full of them. What once had been a borough of largely middle-class Jewish residents had changed by the '70s to a mix of Jews and minority residents, many of them poor.

His future wife, Judith Steinberg, was in the class behind him. They met, so the story goes, when they noticed each other doing crossword puzzles in class. Dr. Stephen E. Goldstone, a Manhattan surgeon, says he knew Dean fairly well, because his roommate was dating Steinberg's roommate, and so the couples and their friends were thrown together. Goldstone says the fact that Dean had been in the workforce set him apart from the other students.

"For him, it was a conscious decision to abandon his career

and commit to medicine," Goldstone says. "He had an exceptional level of commitment and maturity, and he had a calming ability. Things did not bother him the way they did some of the rest of us." In his recollection of Dean the medical student, Goldstone uses descriptives virtually identical to those of Dean's far-flung Yale and St. George's classmates: "He was absolutely a straight-shooter," says Goldstone. "There was never a wall around him, nothing phony."

Dean graduated from medical school in 1978, having taken advantage of an accelerated program at Einstein that enabled students to graduate in three years instead of the usual four. With the rest of his classmates, he anxiously counted down to Match Day, when academic medical centers around the country post the names of students accepted for residency training. Dean matched at his fourth choice; the first three were teaching hospitals in New York City. But the Match decreed otherwise. Dr. Howard Dean, intern, was ordered to report for duty on July 1, 1978, at the Medical Center Hospital of Vermont in Burlington.

Irene Wielawski

Dr. Howard Dean and his wife,
Dr. Judith Steinberg,
share a light moment.
(AP Photo)

CHAPTER 3

A Doctor and a Legislator

The timing of Howard Dean's arrival in Vermont could not have been better. Had he come a decade earlier, the windows of political opportunity would have been nowhere near so numerous or so wide open.

When Dean arrived in the Green Mountain State in 1978, he was 29 years old, fresh out of medical school and ready to begin his residency at the teaching hospital of the University of Vermont in Burlington. An old port city, Burlington begins at water's edge — in this case the eastern shore of Lake Champlain. From there it rises along a long hill to the University of Vermont, the school founded in the 18th century by Ira Allen, brother of Ethan Allen of Green Mountain Boys fame. UVM (the initials of *Universitas Verdes Montes* — University of the Green Mountains in Latin) is Vermont's only publicly funded university and is closely affiliated with the state's largest medical center, where Dean would do his residency.

The Vermont of the late 1970s was a place that had been profoundly altered by the political and social movements of the Vietnam War years. Before 1960, the state's claim to political fame was as a bastion of Republicanism. Vermont and Maine were the only states to vote for Alf Landon against Franklin D.

Roosevelt in 1936, an event that prompted that uniquely Yankee bit of drollery: "As goes Maine, so goes Vermont."

But Vermont's Republicanism was a very moderate — and practical — form, the kind that sent men like George Aiken to the U.S. Senate. Aiken, the former governor who wound up serving in the Senate for 34 years, had caught the nation's attention during the Vietnam War with his comment that the United States should simply "declare victory and get out." Sen. Robert Stafford, another Vermont Republican, was a chief author of the federal Clean Air Act. With Republicans like that, there had been no urgent demand for a Democratic Party, and, as a result, there was not much of a Democratic Party in Vermont.

The political status quo, moderate though it was, had been entrenched for a long time when, in 1962, an affluent, patrician transplant from Massachusetts named Philip Hoff breathed fire into the Democratic Party with a roaring, exuberant victory in the governor's race. The win put into play the notion that Vermont actually could become a two-party state. Hoff, a lawyer, had a Kennedy-like charisma that appealed to a swarm of enthusiastic young voters from the Burlington area, who treated him like royalty on election night, complete with a crown on his head as he perched on the back seat of a convertible for his victory ride. It wouldn't be much of a stretch to suggest that Hoff paved the way for Dean, although the very liberal Hoff, who later served in the state senate, would be a frequent critic of Dean's tightfisted approach to spending on social programs.

> But Vermont's Republicanism was a very moderate — and practical — form, the kind that sent men like George Aiken to the U.S. Senate.

But patricians weren't the only ones coming to town in those years. By 1970, Vermont was known nationally as a hot spot for anti-war organizing, primarily on the campuses of colleges such as Middlebury, Goddard and the University of

Vermont. Goddard, a small campus in the central Vermont town of Plainfield, long had been a haven for radicals and free thinkers, but now the students were taking it off campus and into the community. At Middlebury, kids from upper-middle-class families with expensive boarding-school educations were turning their backs on their parents and their affluent upbringing. Their activism got the attention — not all of it friendly — of Vermonters who historically had been more interested in dairy subsidies than military spending. At the same time, the more rural parts of the state were drawing small groups of political dropouts, disaffected young people who wanted nothing more than to grow organic vegetables, milk goats and live communally outside the mainstream of American life.

By 1975, the Vietnam War had officially ended, and the commune movement of peace, love and harmony had all but disintegrated as its practitioners grew up and got jobs, but the people it had attracted were in Vermont to stay. The hippies who stayed on the land and actually learned to farm got to know some of their native neighbors, who, in turn, came to accept them. Vermonters, pragmatists that they are, tend to live and let live, and so they did in this case.

The anti-war activists formed the core of alternative political parties such as Liberty Union, a small but vocal party comprising radical fringe candidates who railed against government, corporations and anybody else with money. Liberty Union was the first political home of Bernie Sanders, who now holds Vermont's one seat in the U.S. House. A self-declared socialist with a mess of white hair and a Brooklyn accent, Sanders eventually broke with Liberty Union and helped form the Progressive coalition, a group of leftist politicos who have dominated the politics of Burlington since 1981, when Sanders stunned the electorate by squeaking to victory in the mayoral race.

Howard Dean's arrival in Burlington landed him at the epicenter of Vermont's political flux. The little city had emerged as the state's largest city and its financial capital. By 1978 it was well on its way to becoming the city it is today: a trendy little urban area that often shows up on lists of the best places to live. Not only is the city home to the university and the medical center, it also can boast fantastic views of the lake, easy access to sports of every variety, a flourishing arts community and a dozen or more excellent restaurants, all of which is remarkable given that the city's population is only about 40,000 people in a county of 148,000.

However, Burlington was not always the urban garden spot of Vermont. Its history was not that of Yankee farmers but of French-Canadians and Irish who worked in the textile mills powered by the Winooski River. By the 1960s, the mills had gone south or had closed for other reasons, and Burlington looked tired and run-down. The once-prosperous waterfront was lined by abandoned industrial buildings and sagging housing stock that had been built to house the mill workers. The city was in rough shape, and its politics were in the hands of old-line Democrats with Irish names like Hartigan and French-Canadian names like Paquette.

But seeds of change had been sown by Thomas Watson Jr., the chairman of IBM, who had decided around that time to park his new microchip plant next door to Burlington in Essex Junction. IBM not only paid well by Vermont standards, it also brought to town highly educated workers with money to spend. Property values started to rise. Seeing opportunity in the presence of IBM, a group of Burlington's business and political leaders formed an economic development council to recruit other clean, technology-based businesses that would increase the standard of living locally. Burlington was transformed into a vibrant urban center at the heart of an affluent, semi-suburban county that had the added benefit, many people liked to joke, of being so close to Vermont.

When Dean arrived in 1978, the young doctor moved into a cramped second-floor apartment in downtown Burlington. The neighborhood sits on a flat section just before the hill rises steeply to the university. The area historically had been low- and moderate-income family housing, but by the time Dean arrived, students from the university were moving in and landlords were breaking up single-family dwellings into much more lucrative rental apartments.

Dean lived alone at the time: Judith Steinberg, his fiancée, was finishing her last year of medical school at Albert Einstein. One of his neighbors was Esther Sorrell, a Democratic activist who would be hailed as the "Mother of the Democratic Party in Vermont" in her obituary in 1990. Her sister Peggy Hartigan, another active Democrat, lived with her.

Esther's son, William, remembers when Dean first came to town. "I'd stop by my folks' place and my mother would tell me, 'You've got to meet this terrific young doctor,'" recalls Sorrell, who was in private practice with a Burlington law firm at the time. "Howard has said repeatedly that it was my mother who got him involved in politics."

> "Howard was a sponge. He would sit there by the hour, soaking up political history, the gossip, the inside stories . . ."
>
> *William Sorrell,*
> *Friend/Attorney General*

Dean developed a Friday night ritual: He would walk down the block and around the corner to the Sorrells' house. Esther or Peg would have made brownies or chocolate chip cookies. Then the two women and their protégé "would sit down to watch the PBS political shows — *Vermont This Week* [a journalistic roundtable about the week's news] followed by *Washington Week in Review*," says Sorrell, whom Dean later appointed attorney general.

"Howard was a sponge. He would sit there by the hour, soaking up political history, the gossip, the inside stories," Sorrell continues. "He loved all that stuff. I think he was the son my mother always wanted. Howard was much more political than I am." Peg Hartigan served as treasurer for every Howard Dean political campaign until she died in the summer of 1999, the year before Dean's last gubernatorial campaign.

Political Beginning

Sorrell's first clear impressions of Dean were formed when Dean became active in the Citizens' Waterfront Group. Sorrell's firm was representing the city's interests with respect to several issues concerning its aging but potentially lucrative Lake Champlain waterfront. Condominium developers saw gold in the land where abandoned warehouses and an empty railroad station stood. The views across the lake to the Adirondacks of New York would be worth lots of money in the real estate market, but to develop it that way would mean largely shutting the public off from the lakefront.

The committee had been formed to preserve public access to the waterfront, which contained the remnants of the old railroad line in addition to the former mill buildings and run-down housing. The group wanted a public bike path that would allow cycling, walking, jogging and baby strolling close to the water's edge. Dean and Rick Sharp, a local attorney, were the prime movers behind the citizens group. Sharp gives Dean plenty of credit for bull-dogging the issue to a happy outcome. Without Dean, he says, both the bike path and the non-commercial waterfront might never have come about.

> "He managed to quietly repeal an 1876 law that would have given the filled land along the waterfront back to the railroads instead of to the city."
>
> *Rick Sharp,*
> *Bike Path Advocate*

"Howard was the spark plug that made it all happen," says Sharp. "He made the first phone calls. He was very active. One day he'd be out preaching to a senior citizens' group about the importance of preserving a right-of-way. The next day, he'd be out there with his crowbar and his chainsaw, removing railroad ties from the filled land owned by the railroad.

"[Later] when he was in the Legislature, he managed to quietly repeal an 1876 law that would have given the filled land along the waterfront back to the railroads instead of to the city. Our work resulted in two Supreme Court rulings — one U.S. and one Vermont — that became landmark decisions affecting the conversion of old railroad land to bike paths all over the country.

"You have to realize that in the beginning, politicians were laughing at us with our idea of a bike path and a public waterfront. It was complete pie-in-the-sky."

Sorrell was equally impressed. "Here's this guy who comes from away — he's a doctor, and doctors are busy people — he's doing his residency, he's volunteering his time at a low-income medical clinic, and he's giving all this time to the citizens' committee," says Sorrell, shaking his head. "Somehow, this guy seems to survive without any sleep. You have to remember, this was long before the Energizer bunny."

In 1979, Judith Steinberg moved into the little apartment on Converse Court and joined Dean in the hospital's residency program. If they had a social life, nobody seemed to notice. Then, as now, they didn't party or make the social rounds. Sorrell says they used the little bit of leisure time they had to bike, hike, ski and canoe, all of which have been favorite pastimes throughout the years.

In 1981, Howard and Judith were married in a ceremony in Manhattan. That was the same year that Dean, a family practitioner, opened his medical practice in Shelburne, an affluent bedroom community of Burlington. His wife joined him in the practice in 1985 after completing her residency at Medical Center Hospital and at a hospital in Montreal. Dean would keep his practice for the next decade, literally until the day he became governor in 1991.

At the same time, though, politics was pulling at Dean. Esther Sorrell had signed him up to work on Jimmy Carter's presidential re-election campaign in 1980. William Sorrell remembers that Dean was among the campaign's hardest-working volunteers. "He never had an attitude about what he was asked to do," Sorrell recalls. "If he was asked to lick stamps, he licked stamps. He never said, 'I'm a doctor so don't ask me to lick stamps.' He was always willing to do whatever was required."

Burlington politics at the time were an internecine mess. Garrison Nelson, a political scientist at the University of Vermont and a trenchant observer of the political scene, ascribes the dissension to the rise of Bernie Sanders. When Sanders became mayor of Burlington in 1981 by a mere 10 votes, Nelson says, "city Democrats panicked. They were all at each other's throats. The French were the social conservatives, the Irish were a little more moderate, and then there was Bernie and his people, burning down the house. It got ugly. Esther advised Howard to stay out of it, so he did."

Instead of entering local politics in Burlington, he set sights on the legislature. Vermont's General Assembly was — and is — a citizen legislature. Lawmakers are expected to have jobs in the real world, not to earn their livings from being legislators. The session lasts five months, give or take. The lawmakers convene at the state capital of Montpelier in early January, spend four days a week on the business of state, and go home for the year in spring, preferably well before Memorial Day. The short schedule meant that Dean could be a House member while still practicing medicine. In 1982, with the strong backing of Esther Sorrell and company, he ran as a

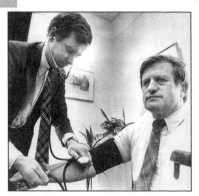

Lt. Gov. Howard Dean takes the blood pressure of state senator Douglas Baker in Dean's office at the Statehouse.
(AP Photo by Toby Talbot)

Democrat for the Vermont House seat from Ward 2, the district that included his apartment.

Dean's platform for his House campaign consisted largely of his support for the Burlington bike path and his determination to protect the city's waterfront from aggressive development. Although the issues primarily affected Burlington and Chittenden County, the bike path needed both federal and state funding to succeed. Sorrell says that issue, combined with his volunteer work in a low-income medical clinic, gave Dean broad appeal across the changing demographics of his district. Yuppies, who wanted the bike path, and low-income voters all liked him. "Howard got both votes," Sorrell explains. "He won easily."

The legislature, too, was a political body in transition, and that was largely because of a legislator by the name of Ralph Wright, an old-style Irish-American pol with a strong Boston accent, who had come to the House in 1981. Unlike some of the older House members who considered politics a gentlemen's game, Wright introduced a bare-knuckles style of politics predicated on wheeling and dealing. Wright rose to become the Democratic leader and then Speaker of the House, and he tapped Paul Poirier, a high school teacher and hockey coach from the blue-collar city of Barre to be his assistant — to count votes and keep fellow Democrats in line. Wright's aggressive tactics unnerved many of the older legislators, who didn't quite understand the new rules of the game. Until the advent of Wright and company, state politics had been largely an old boys' club. People were unfailingly polite to each other, and civility was expected. But now the old collegial way of doing business was washing out to sea, and nobody knew quite what was coming in on the new tide.

In January 1983, Wright and Poirier were just beginning their second terms in the House, and Howard Dean was a freshman.

"He didn't make waves; he was friendly to everybody, and he was loyal to the caucus," recalls Poirier, who now lobbies on behalf of a mental-health advocacy group. "Clearly, he loved politics, and he was always asking, 'What can I do to help?'

"We didn't actually see all that much of him because he still had his medical practice. He'd get to the Statehouse right before we started, and he'd often leave early to see patients. Ralph and I nicknamed him 'Ho-Ho' — we always called him that. We'd look around and say, 'When's Ho-Ho coming in today?' Nobody could ever find Ho-Ho."

In all probability, nobody could find Dean because his life was so busy. He was practicing internal medicine in a converted barn in Shelburne while remaining active in Burlington politics. In addition, he volunteered his time at the low-income medical clinic in Burlington's Old North End, a neighborhood that has resisted all attempts at gentrification. Newly married, Dean had a wife whose interest in politics was less than zero. And soon the two Deans would become a family of four — Anne was born in 1984, followed by Paul in 1986.

"The real tug in his life has always been the conflicting pull of family life and politics," says Bob Sherman, a bearded grizzly bear of a man who dwarfs the clean-cut Dean when they stand together. Sherman played football against Dean at boarding school, but got to know him only when Dean was a freshman legislator and Sherman was a Statehouse reporter for the *Rutland Herald* and its sister paper the *Times-Argus* in Barre and Montpelier.

"In those early years, I don't believe Howard had any close friends other than his old roommates from Yale and his buddies from boarding school," says David Wolk, an educator and one of Dean's closest friends in Vermont. "He and Judy never socialized, either with politicians or with doctors. They don't go out to movies; they don't go out to dinner, and they don't party. . . . Howard's life was very compartmentalized — he had his political life, he had his medical practice, and he had his family.

LEARNING TO MANEUVER

Dean was re-elected to the House in 1984 and his political skills were being noticed. He was one of the first politicians to make use of public access television, and, with no training, he demonstrated an innate ability to watch the clock and end exactly on time. "It was like he instinctively knew how to be a TV producer," said one Dean talk-show guest. The 1984 election also revealed another side of the man that his political cronies hadn't seen before: an ability to size up political competition quickly and outmaneuver them. Like a hawk, Dean can circle calmly, biding his time, then swoop down swiftly to hit his target.

Howard Dean reads to his children, Paul and Anne, at home in Burlington.
(Photo by Craig Line)

As the 1984 legislative campaigns began unfolding that fall, Ralph Wright planned to run for House speaker, and Poirier, Wright's side-kick, wanted to become the minority leader. But Republicans in the House held a majority and were expected to retain it, and chances were good Wright would end up minority leader for another term and Poirier would have to seek re-election to his old job as minority whip. Hence, Poirier was mightily surprised when a colleague told him that Howard Dean — campaigning for his second legislative term — also was quietly recruiting support for his own bid to be minority whip. Poirier was angry.

"I was at a forum when a friend told me, 'Paul, I got a call from this guy named Howard Dean saying he was going to run for minority whip,'" Poirier remembers. "I was livid. I got home that night at about 11, and there was a message on my machine from Howard informing me of his plans. I returned his call immediately. I remember he was surprised to hear from me at that hour. He was sort of stammering on the other end of the line, saying, 'Well, Paul, I didn't think you were running for the job.'

"I told him, 'If you do this, Howard, you'll lose, and I guarantee that you'll end up on the Fish and Wildlife Committee for the rest of your career,'" that committee being a political dead zone for a representative from an urban area.

Wright and Poirier surprisingly got their promotions, and Dean ascended to minority whip. Wright believes that if Dean had not won as whip he would have moved on to some interest or challenge other than politics.

"The world wouldn't have been 'according to Howard,'" Wright wrote in his political memoir, *All Politics Is Personal*. "He probably would have tired of the legislature and either returned to his full-time practice or ventured off searching for another political level to make a re-entry," says Wright. What it does show, according to Wright, is that Dean "has no fear of losing." He says Dean seemed to think that politics is important but it makes no sense to become attached to the political life or take it too seriously. "If someone has to lose (and he never believed for a moment it would be him), one just pulled the sheet up over his or her head and moved on to the next bed."

LIEUTENANT GOVERNOR

Dean's next bed proved to be bigger than the last, and again it was achieved partly as a result of serendipity. By 1986 when the next elections rolled around, the Deans had two small children and a full-time medical practice in Shelburne. They had moved out of their apartment and bought a modest house in Burlington, a raised ranch with a shady yard near the lake. "You'd know it by the rusty mailbox at the bottom of the driveway," says Wolk.

The move had taken Dean out of his House district and into one already represented by two loyal Democrats. Wright and Poirier warned Dean that he would lose their support if he challenged the incumbents. So the question became: What next?

While there are a few conflicts in the many versions of what happened next, most agree that Dean — somewhat remarkably, given the fact that he was still new to politics — seriously considered challenging Rep. James Jeffords for Vermont's one seat in the U.S. House. Jeffords was a moderate-to-liberal Republican who voted with the Democrats as often as he voted with his own party. His maverick politics played well in

Vermont, and his support ran deep and wide throughout the state, particularly among those voters who claimed no party affiliation. Jeffords had been the state's attorney general before entering the U.S. House. He would have been an extremely tough incumbent to beat.

> "There are three things you have to understand about Howard Dean: He's aggressive, he's politically astute and he's lucky."
>
> *Bob Sherman,*
> *Montpelier Lobbyist*

Bob Sherman sees Dean's boldness as evidence of the fact that "he's an aggressive political animal, plus he's a physician trained to make life-and-death decisions on the spot and believe in those decisions. He has high self-esteem, high ambition and he believes in his intellect."

In the end, Dean didn't challenge Jeffords, but that same aggressiveness, coupled with his instinct for opportunity, surfaced in his decision to run for lieutenant governor that year. Gov. Madeleine Kunin, a Democrat, was finishing her first two-year term at the time, and Republican Lt. Gov. Peter Smith also was expected to run for re-election.

Suddenly, the political winds shifted. "Bernie (Sanders) threw his hat into the governor's race," says Garrison Nelson, "and as soon as Bernie announced, Peter Smith jumped in, sensing that Madeleine would be vulnerable in a three-way race." The game of musical chairs at the top left open the lieutenant governor's seat. Although Poirier was again the obvious candidate for the opening, Dean leaped into the fray ahead of Poirier and announced he would run. Although Poirier insists Dean had his blessing, Bob Sherman isn't so sure that was the case. "As I see it, Howard leapfrogged over Paul again," says Sherman. "There are three things you have to understand about Howard Dean: He's aggressive, he's politically astute and he's lucky."

What made him particularly lucky in 1986 was a massive Democratic win in Vermont, spearheaded by Sen. Patrick

Leahy's victory. Partly because of Leahy's coattails, Kunin retained her office, and Dean got to be lieutenant governor, defeating a Republican legislator named Susan Auld virtually while no one was looking. Immediately, Dean tapped Jane Williams, a neighbor and a former Kunin aide, to be his one and only staff person. Williams remained with him until she retired from the governor's office in August 2001.

Because the lieutenant governor presides over the Senate, Dean needed to make the attitudinal leap from the scrappy, partisan politics of the House to the smaller, more collegial atmosphere of the Senate. "He was the new guy in town. The change of style took a bit of learning," says Williams, "but Howard was a quick learner. He loves the political process and getting things done, and the things that got through the Senate were important to him — health care bills, natural resources legislation."

His basically middle-of-the road political sensibilities allowed him to forge alliances with moderate Republicans, who were more common in the Senate than in the House. "I have to laugh now when he's portrayed as a radical liberal," says Williams. "I don't think the liberal left was always the most comfortable place for him to be."

The other aspect of his personality that has always pulled him to the right is his reluctance to spend money, either politically or privately. Hence, he often opposed the liberals on spending for social programs. Nor would he spend any money on himself.

> The other aspect of his personality that has always pulled him to the right is his reluctance to spend money, either politically or privately.

"He's pretty thrifty," admits Williams. "As lieutenant governor, he scheduled himself for 30 to 40 hours a week in his medical practice, and I scheduled him for another 40 or 50 hours as lieutenant governor. In between all that, he'd paint his own house rather than hire someone to do it for him. And while he was painting, he'd sit the kids down on the front porch and tell them a story."

Because the lieutenant governor's office budget was so small, Williams was his Gal Friday, his personal assistant, as well as his friend. She and her husband, Tony, had moved into a house on the same street as Dean in the same year that the Deans moved in. The only way to make the frantic pace work was to keep a tight schedule. "Judy had the schedule, Tony had the schedule and I had the schedule," remembers Williams. "That way, if Howard was off in Bennington (nearly three hours' drive from Burlington) and Judy was seeing patients, Tony would pick the kids up from day care."

The flip side, she says, was that "he was a wonderful boss to work for. He acted as his own office manager, his own scheduler, his own press guy. He'd let me know exactly what he wanted me to do, and I did it. I could tell he had been brought up right — he always said thank you. If one of my kids was home . . . he'd tell me to take the day off. I don't think I ever had a birthday without a card made by Howard, Judy and the kids."

In that fast-paced first term, Dean and Williams scrambled to host a meeting, at a downtown hotel, of the National Association of Lieutenant Governors, a legacy of Peter Smith's tenure. "It was wild," says Williams. "We had no money to run the thing, so we had to fund-raise as well as organize all the meetings and a state dinner. There were 55 lieutenant governors [50 states and 5 territories] and their staff people, plus a lot of corporate types. It was a lot of fun, but it nearly killed us."

Dean's run for re-election two years later was a walk in the park. His opponent was an obscure Republican named Pan Zolotis. No one in Vermont politics had ever heard of the man before the 1988 election season, and no one has heard of him since.

Then, two years later, the door appeared to be opening once more. Gov. Kunin decided not to run for re-election, leaving the Democratic Party without an obvious contender. Running for governor seemed like a good option until Republican Richard

Snelling, who had served four terms in the 1970s and early 1980s before retiring from politics, decided to try for a fifth term. Snelling was popular with voters, and Dean chose to remain in the second spot.

Yet again, he made the right choice. Snelling defeated the Democrat, and Dean stayed right where he was, biding his time and learning all he could from Snelling, a man he greatly admired. Again Dean was not destined to stand still for long. He began his third term as lieutenant governor in January 1991. Less than nine months later, on a hot summer morning, Snelling was found dead near his backyard swimming pool, the victim of a heart attack.

Sally West Johnson

Lt. Gov. Howard Dean is sworn in as governor by Supreme Court Chief Justice Fred Allen on August 14, 1991, following the death of Gov. Richard Snelling.
(AP Photo by Craig Line)

CHAPTER 4

Unexpectedly, He's Governor

Tuesday morning, August 14, 1991, began routinely enough. Howard Dean, physician and part-time lieutenant governor, awoke, dressed, ate breakfast, kissed his two children goodbye and headed for the medical office in Shelburne that he shared with his wife and another doctor.

Dean arrived for work at 8 a.m. and soon was seeing his first patient of the day, when the receptionist rushed into the examination room to tell him he had an urgent phone call. The message, from another patient, would end Dean's career as a physician and launch him into a new one as governor of Vermont. Howard Dean would hold the office for nearly eleven and one-half years, the second-longest governorship in the state's history.

Though he had served two terms in the Vermont House of Representatives and three as lieutenant governor, Dean was considered a relatively minor figure, almost a lightweight, in Vermont politics on that day in August. Especially when compared with the man who had been governor for the previous eight months. Republican Richard Snelling, 64, had become a revered figure. He had come back as governor after serving four terms in the late 1970s and early '80s. A millionaire businessman, who retired from politics in part to spend time sailing his boat on the ocean, Snelling found that he missed the political life, so, with approval of the voters, he returned to the governorship in 1990. His first order of business was to reduce the huge budget deficit that accumulated under the watch of his predecessor, Democratic Gov. Madeleine Kunin.

By August 1991, Snelling's formula of tax increases and budget cuts had pointed the way toward fiscal health, and Snelling was receiving widespread credit for his efforts. Dean, by contrast, had remained in the shadows. The main duty of Vermont's lieutenant governor is to preside over the Senate during the four or five months each winter and spring that the legislature is in session. Dean also had his family and medical practice to keep

Gov. Howard Dean joins Hillary Clinton in Woodstock, Vermont, on June 19, 1993.
(Rutland Herald *Photo by Vyto Starinskas*)

him busy and out of the limelight. Dean's most recent mention in the Vermont newspapers was in a story on new poll results, which also appeared on that fateful morning of August 14. "Democratic Lt. Gov. Howard Dean outstripped other Vermont politicians for anonymity," the Associated Press reported. "Dean has been elected to statewide office three times, but 39 percent of those questioned had no opinion of him or had not heard of him."

"It was one of those things that was so ironic about that day," longtime Dean aide Kate O'Connor recalls. "Here's a poll that shows nobody knows who he is."

That would soon change.

The phone call for Dean that morning was from another patient, who wanted to pass on this message overheard on a police scanner: Emergency personnel were responding to

Snelling's home in Shelburne, just a few miles away from Dean's office. The governor was dead.

"I hyperventilated," Dean recalled later in an interview. But he soon got his breathing back under control. "I went back and finished the physical. I figured that, later, I'd have a hard time fitting it in," he said.

Another call came a few minutes later, this one from one of Snelling's aides. Dean was told formally that he should prepare to assume the office of governor. Dean asked his medical partners to take responsibility for the rest of the patients he was to see that day, and began making his own phone calls.

The medical examiner's report said Snelling had died many hours before — most likely the previous afternoon or evening — after suffering a heart attack while cleaning his swimming pool. His body had lain through the night by the edge of the pool. Snelling had been scheduled to meet two magazine writers for an interview at a diner that morning. Two state police drivers had gone to his house to pick him up, but when the governor didn't follow his custom of immediately answering the door, they went around the house and found his body. Snelling's wife, Barbara, was in Buffalo on business. New York Gov. Mario Cuomo provided a state helicopter to fly the new widow home to Vermont.

Dean stayed for a while in his medical office in part because that office had three phone lines, while the lieutenant governor's office in Montpelier had only two. When his young children heard the news, they couldn't grasp the tragic circumstances — they cried because it meant their dad would be too busy to go on the planned family vacation. Dean also made calls to a succession of political allies, lobbyists and friends. "I need you to get down to the Statehouse immediately," he told them.

ADVISERS SUMMONED

"I needed to surround myself with people I knew and trusted," Dean said in an interview with the *Rutland Herald* about a week after he became governor. "I couldn't worry about the public perceptions about whether this was the lobbyists getting in the door, or whether this was the Kunin administration or something. I had to get competence, I had to get quality, I had to get people who had been through [similar crises] before, because I hadn't."

One of Kunin's goals, aside from increasing state aid to education and protecting the environment, had been to promote women to the top echelons of state government. Two of the women who had worked for Kunin were among the first people Dean called. Kathy Hoyt had served as Kunin's chief of staff. Her experience and empathetic grace would make her a source of calm in the storm. Kate O'Connor, who had grown up in a political family in Brattleboro, had worked both for Kunin and in a Dean re-election campaign. Early on, she had demonstrated a dependability that would soon morph into indispensability. She would later serve as a key aide in his gubernatorial and presidential campaigns.

> "I had to get competence, I had to get quality, I had to get people who had been through this before, because I hadn't."
>
> *Howard Dean,*
> *New Governor*

Hoyt wasn't sure Dean was ready for the governor's job. "He didn't want to be governor when the kids were so young," she says. Both children were under 10; Dean was happy where he was, "and this job was thrust upon him," Hoyt says.

By the time Dean left Shelburne and made the 50-minute drive to Montpelier, the tiny, two-room lieutenant governor's office on the first floor of Vermont's tidy, gold-domed Statehouse was already crowded. Arriving soon after Dean was Bob Sherman, the affable lobbyist and former newspaper reporter, who had played football against Dean in high school. Sherman also had done a stint as press secretary to Kunin before he went on to found a lobbying firm with another former Kunin aide. The firm of Kimbell, Sherman & Ellis had become one of Vermont's most influential lobbying shops.

Montpelier, the nation's smallest state capital, isn't anyone's idea of a fashion center even during the winter and spring, when the legislature is in town. In the summer, ties on men are rare. Sherman had gone to work that morning in shorts and a T-shirt. "It wasn't really appropriate," he says. Lacking the time to make the 25-mile trip on back roads home to change, Sherman dashed to Stevens & Co., a men's clothing store on Main Street, and got himself outfitted for the somber occasion.

When Dean arrived in Montpelier to be sworn in as governor, he also wasn't appropriately attired. "The first thing we had to do was to get Howard dressed," Sherman says. He dispatched Anya Rader, who would become a top health care policy adviser for Dean, to buy the governor a crisp white shirt and a tie. "There was this furious effort to write this [speech]," Rader recalls. "And I remember heading down to Stevens to get a shirt and tie that would look good."

Dean took charge of the situation when he arrived at his Statehouse office, assigning tasks to those present. More phone calls had to be made. Appointments had to be scheduled with top Snelling aides. Dean was described as calm but on edge. "We were all in awe of what we were going to be doing in the next few days," Sherman says. With the doctor on the scene, it took on the aura of a political and governmental emergency room.

INAUGURATION SPEECH

Sherman had written speeches for Kunin, and when he reached the Statehouse, he fell into his old role. Dean sent him to the nearby offices of *Vermont Life* magazine, a state publication, where he would join the magazine's editor in drafting Dean's inauguration speech to be delivered that afternoon.

"The speech had to be respectful of Snelling's legacy. It had to be respectful of Barbara Snelling. And it had to say what [Dean] was going to do . . . without sounding like Al Haig," Sherman says, referring to President Ronald Reagan's secretary of state, who famously claimed he was in charge after the president was shot outside a Washington hotel in 1981. "Snelling was a really powerful figure, a beloved figure in Vermont politics," Sherman says. "It was tough."

More than 100 people gathered in the governor's ceremonial office that afternoon as Dean delivered what he still regards as one of his best speeches.

Sadly, the state of Vermont must today say farewell to Governor Richard Snelling. . . . I personally mourn his passing. Richard Snelling was a consummate leader, a man of great energy and presence, who spent more than 30 years serving people in the state. Since his election last year, Governor Snelling led our state through some of the most difficult economic times in our history. His leadership and vision put Vermont on a path to financial responsibility that I intend to do my best to follow. . . . I have met this afternoon with Governor Snelling's personal staff and cabinet. I have asked them to continue doing their jobs through this very difficult time. . . .

Kathy Hoyt recalled later, "It worked. It comforted people that we weren't making major changes . . . that we were carrying on with Snelling's agenda, the agenda we had been given."

The Snelling agenda was one that the moderate Democrat could embrace. It called for frugality, something that was not just part of Dean's theory of governing but also part of his character. The first priority was to balance the state's budget. Snelling's plan of fiscal austerity and temporary tax increases appeared to fit the task.

Then there were the personal, and personnel, issues. "I think we did the right thing," Hoyt says, by "assuring everybody on Snelling's staff that we would find them places to stay." Dean kept on four of five Snelling cabinet members and many other top managers. "The difficulty about this is that I actually have to neglect my own party," Dean said in an interview at the time. "I've got to reach out to Republicans, and I've got to reach out to the business community and convince them the place isn't going to fall apart."

One Republican whose advice Dean sought was Bill Gilbert, who had served at one time as Snelling's general counsel and later as his administration secretary, traditionally the most political of cabinet posts and always occupied by the governor's closest aide.

"Dean invited me to come over and, in a public way, meet with him to discuss the transition, and that happened the next day," Gilbert recalls. "It is important, when you have that kind of shocking transition, to show that Vermonters can pull together and support the governor, regardless of the fact that I am a Republican. Howard handled that transition with grace and real sensitivity. He was very thoughtful and generous."

Gov. Howard Dean gestures to a crowd before tapping a maple tree in St. Albans, Vermont, on a February day in 1992.
(AP Photo by Craig Line)

Dean also tapped another of Montpelier's most influential lawyer-lobbyists, David M. Wilson, to be his administration secretary, the chief budget and day-to-day operations officer in state government. Wilson, as a lobbyist, was both pragmatic and apolitical, working well with both Democrats and Republicans in the legislature. He had served in both the Snelling and Kunin administrations. His appointment by Dean — Wilson agreed to serve for a year and then return to his much more lucrative lobbying practice — sent a signal of bipartisanship.

The first days of the new administration were frenetic. Dean scheduled 15- or 30-minute meetings with a host of top Snelling aides, asking questions and hearing them out on the issues facing their segments of state government.

"The precision that he exhibited in interviewing people, hour after hour, day after day, was extraordinary," says Glenn Gershaneck, who held high-ranking posts under Snelling and then Dean. "He categorized each situation . . . then the connections would click in his head . . . and then he'd find a thread." Dean would interview each with care and then determine where each would fit best in the administration. "It was extraordinary to watch," says Gershaneck.

Before Snelling's death, the headlines of the state's papers were dominated by news of impending crises in Israel, a significant Rutland drug bust, the aftermath of the first Persian Gulf War. Then all eyes were on Snelling's death and the arrival of the new Dean administration, and after about three weeks a sense of normalcy returned to the state. The pause in attention gave the fledgling chief executive some breathing room.

Dean and his staff had spent their first days working out of the governor's ceremonial office in the Statehouse, but after about a week he moved down the street to the governor's larger quarters in a state office building, which had a commanding view of the Statehouse and the wooded hillside behind it. It was a month before Dean felt comfortable enough to put his own books on the office shelves and place pictures of his family on the desk that had been used by Snelling.

> "One of my most persistent activities during the early '90's was trying to fend off the more liberal wing of the Democratic Party."
>
> *Glenn Gershaneck,*
> *Former Press Secretary*

In addition to former Snelling aides, Dean surrounded himself with several utility lobbyists, and in that context, his first major decision was not surprising.

Vermont's power companies had been trying to win

approval for a 25-year contract to purchase electricity from Hydro-Quebec, the utility owned and operated by the province of Quebec. It was a deal designed to satisfy about one-third of the state's needs. But it also was a deal that was coming under increasing criticism from environmental groups, which opposed Hydro-Quebec's huge dam projects on wild rivers in the northern part of the province, and by human-rights groups, which were concerned about the fate of the province's Cree Indians, who would be flooded off their land. Also, in the weeks before Snelling's death, some consumer groups were raising serious questions about whether such a power purchase actually would be a good deal for Vermont. New York was backing out of a similar contract with the Quebec utility.

But Vermont's power companies were eager to seal the deal; and, in the first of many decisions that would anger liberal Democrats, Dean announced he would support it. The deal's critics would turn out to be right. In the late 1990s, Vermont's two biggest power companies nearly became insolvent as they struggled to pay what turned out to be high costs for Quebec power. The board that regulates utilities eventually approved steep rate increases for consumers, and Vermont business leaders later complained loudly that the state's high electric rates hurt their ability to compete.

That Dean became governor in August rather than in the middle of the legislative session gave him some time before the Legislature would convene. It gave his team time to establish a government, plan a transition, make a budget proposal and formulate other legislative priorities. It also gave them an extended honeymoon, one that would last through Dean's first legislative session as governor. The honeymoon would be his last — at least with many legislators in his own party.

"One of my most persistent activities during the early '90s was trying to fend off the more liberal wing of the Democratic Party," says Gershanek, who became Dean's press secretary before eventually heading the state Transportation Agency. "The will to spend money always exceeded the resources available, and the push to spend came mostly from the left."

Dean's agenda that first session was designed to be modest and, above all, financially sound.

"I think his key issues — that all children have health care, that land be conserved, that transportation is improved — were all there at the beginning," Kathy Hoyt explains. "But you can't do anything if the money isn't there, and he understood that. We decided in the first couple of weeks what we'd be pushing for. And on top of that list was fiscal responsibility."

That first session opened on January 7, 1992, five months after Snelling had died and eight months before Dean had to stand for his first election as governor. Expectations were muted, emotions were raw, and all eyes were on the un-elected governor when he delivered his State of the State address.

The broad themes had been hashed out during the early winter with his advisers. He pledged to reform welfare, repair Vermont's potholed roads and highways, protect open space, help farmers, improve health care and work to reduce child abuse. And to do it within the fiscal framework laid down by Snelling.

All of this surprised no one. But Dean ended his speech with an uncharacteristic departure from pragmatism, indulging in a rare emotional appeal to his audience.

We are a state, which truly is a family, a family with a heritage of respect for each other, regardless of our differences. I ask you to remember and sustain these values as you deliberate. Respect for the land, respect for each other, caring and love. With these values, we will prevail.

Darren Allen

Gov. Howard Dean in 2001 reports on a
state survey that determined that just over
51,000 Vermonters have no
health insurance. That's roughly
8.5 percent of the state's population,
about half the national rate.
(AP Photo by Toby Talbot)

CHAPTER 5

Fiscally Tight, but Not Always

Nord Brue scheduled the formal opening of Franklin Foods' expanded cheese manufacturing plant in Enosburg for what turned out to be a gorgeous fall day in 1993. Brue, a Burlington businessman, was also developing the Bruegger's chain of bagel shops; he and his partners had invested several million dollars in the Enosburg plant, a cluster of low-slung white and blue buildings near a sweeping curve of the Missisquoi River. The facility was a big deal for Enosburg, a small town near the Canadian border. As many as 60 people would be added to the firm's work force.

As the town selectmen and other local dignitaries gathered at the plant entrance at mid-morning, Gov. Howard Dean's car pulled into the parking lot. Dean shook hands all around and made a few remarks, brief but clearly heartfelt. "It's just great what you're doing here," Dean said. "You folks are doing a terrific job. Keep it up."

The governor's appearance meant a lot to Brue. Getting to Enosburg wasn't all that easy: The town is a good two-hour drive from the governor's office in Montpelier, along two-lane roads that wander through what seems like endless farm country. Many people live their whole lives in Vermont and never get to Enosburg. Yet Dean had not hesitated when Brue asked him to come. "I'd go a long way to get a new industry to come to Vermont," Brue remembers him saying, "and I don't know why I shouldn't go just as far to keep one here."

Brue knew the visit wasn't just a favor to him. Dean was a governor after his own heart; he considered him a real departure for Vermont, a state that elected a socialist to Congress. Tough environmental laws, relatively high tax rates and generous welfare benefits, plus the anti-business bias of some elements of the newly powerful Democratic Party had contrived to give the state something of an anti-business air.

"Howard understands economic reality," Brue says, explaining why he has supported Dean so enthusiastically. "He's economically literate. He's like Clinton in that regard. He knew he would have to grow the economy to be able to do the things he wanted to do. He also knew that if the Vermont income tax rate rose, he could not attract or retain business in the state."

Brue chuckles about the national perception of Dean as a liberal and an environmentalist. "He's a guy who wants to do things," Brue says. "That's where his friends on the green side will be surprised. He'll make tradeoffs. If they are expecting a perfectly green world — that's not Howard."

Brue is just one person, of course, but he is an unusually thoughtful one, and his views reflect those of the Vermont business community, which in general supported Dean strongly during his nearly eleven and one-half years as governor. It did so primarily because of his conservative management of the state's budget and his efforts to hold down, and even reduce, the state's income tax rates. When Dean left office in early 2003, most states were in dire financial shape, their revenues hammered by the collapse of the dot-com economy. Vermont, by contrast, had a comfortable surplus, thanks largely to Dean.

CLOSING THE CHECKBOOK

Dean took office in an atmosphere of shock and sadness after Gov. Richard Snelling's death. An untested member of the other party, Dean was thrust into the governor's job with little preparation and no warning. Such a precipitous shift is challenging enough, but the situation Dean faced was particularly difficult. The state was in financial straits, and Snelling, who had taken office just eight months earlier, barely had his arms around the problem. He was facing a deficit that ran to some $65 million, a huge number for a fiscally conservative state. Under Gov. Madeleine Kunin, budgets had risen by 60 percent. And as her tenure was coming to a close, the economy was sinking into recession, which cut sharply into state revenues. This situation was troubling to Democrats, horrifying to Republicans.

Snelling, who was both a conservative business executive and a philosopher of government, had designed a strategy to get the state back on track. First, he resolved to peg state expenditure increases to the long-term growth rate of the Vermont economy. His financial analysts told him that rate was 4.12 percent. He was also determined, however, not to carve so deeply into state government that it could not carry out its responsibilities. That meant he had to get more money quickly.

So he went to Ralph Wright, the powerful Democratic speaker of the Vermont House. Wright dominated the Statehouse in those days. He and his chief lieutenant, Paul Poirier, had provided the muscle for the enactment of a long skein of progressive legislation put forward by Kunin, covering issues from education to health care to the environment.

> "Howard understands economic reality. He's economically literate."
>
> *Nord Brue,*
> *Burlington Businessman*

Wright was a genuine liberal Democrat; he didn't lose much sleep over the travails of the business community, and he believed the more help government could provide to the environment and working people the better. He also wanted to get as much money for this as he could from the wealthy, which meant increasing the progressivity of the state income tax. The Vermont income tax is set as a percentage of a person's federal tax, which makes it easy to calculate. That percentage, which is the same for rich and poor, runs in the mid-20s. A progressive state tax would assess higher rates for the well-off and lower ones for the less well-off.

In his political memoir, *All Politics Is Personal,* Wright describes how Snelling came to him one afternoon during the spring legislative session and asked for his help. They went out into the empty House chamber and sat in a couple of adjoining seats. Snelling told him how much he appreciated the way Wright was managing the situation, and then he made his offer.

"'I've thought about all this, so please don't respond until I'm finished,'" Wright recalls Snelling saying. "'I'm here to offer you a progressive income tax. One that puts 28 percent on the lowest rung, 31 percent on the middle group and 34 percent on the richest Vermonters. The one caveat is you've got to promise me we sunset [return] it all back down to the present rate of 25 percent when the deficit is paid. . . . I think it's the fairest way we can go and it's a small thank you for helping me on this.'"

"Life never ceases to surprise me," Wright says in his book, "for here was the governor, my partner, but still my political opponent in the eyes of the world, offering to do what I had only dreamed of doing. I coulda kissed him!"

> The Dean approach rapidly cleaned up the state's fiscal problem. In 1993, the first year that the budget was really Dean's, he actually cut spending for the general fund, the state's main budget, by 2.15 percent.

The deal won approval in the spring and was in effect when Dean took office in August. Dean's approach was to accept the Snelling philosophy of tying state spending to the growth rate of the economy, but Dean, in practice, was far tougher on spending than Snelling ever was. Tom Pelham, who was Dean's budget chief for much of his tenure, says he and Dean calculated that the Snelling budget track was pitched too high by $100 million. So they determined to cut spending even more sharply than Snelling had contemplated.

Pelham watched the progress of Dean's budget management from its early days, and he is still somewhat awed by it. For one thing, Dean wanted his budget guys to be tough — you had to get used to commissioners and department heads wheedling for more money. They were not going to get it from Pelham; he had his orders to stay on the sustainable track of about 4 percent growth, and he was following them. If someone wanted to get past that, he or she had to get past Dean himself.

Pelham refers to these conversations between a governor and his managers as "white couch" events. The governor's office on the fifth floor of the Pavilion, the state office building, is furnished with several white couches. When people come in to see the governor, they sit on the couches. According to Pelham, officials often succeeded in making their case to Kunin that their departments needed more than they had been allotted in the governor's budget.

But there weren't any successful "white couch" events with Dean, according to Pelham. "That never happened to me with Howard Dean," he says. "I was the Darth Vader of the Dean administration."

The Dean approach rapidly cleaned up the state's fiscal problem. In 1993, the first year that the budget was really Dean's, he actually cut spending for the general fund, the state's main budget, by 2.15 percent. In 1994, spending rose by 2.07 percent, but Dean retired the deficit. And from 1995 through 1999, when, as Pelham puts it, the economy was booming and money was coming in "over the gunwales," the Dean general fund rose by an average of 3.71 percent a year, 10 percent *below* the sustainable track. The rainy day (emergency) funds filled to the brim and spilled over. And Dean had "one-time" money to spend for stuff he loved, such as buying wild land to protect it.

Pelham was fascinated by how this discipline was imposed. He recalled the day when Cornelius "Con" Hogan, the secretary of human services and the elder statesman of the cabinet, brought a new senior bureaucrat to the Pavilion to meet the governor and then to attend a budget meeting between the governor, his finance staff and the extended cabinet, all the first- and second-tier bureaucrats who had budgets of their own. Hogan's new manager had been recruited from a regional social services agency; she was a bright, compassionate, committed liberal, like many of the people who populate the state bureaucracy. When she, Hogan and the governor emerged from Dean's office and walked across the hall to the big conference room overlooking the city, they were laughing and talking like old friends.

> The only real exception to rigid budget discipline was health care. "That is where he really put his pedal to the metal."
>
> *Tom Pelham,*
> *Dean's Budget Manager*

Then the meeting started. One budget manager after another got up to plead for increases.

"We really need some more money in this area," one said.

"No," the governor said.

Another manager: "I can't manage this sector without more money."

Dean: "No, we couldn't do that."

Another manager: "We *reeeally* need more money for this."

Howard Dean: "No."

Pelham enjoyed this tableau. He had designed the budget and he wasn't losing a nickel. Dean had read every briefing document, and no one could crack him. His style was also interesting. Kunin and Snelling were immersed in the machinery of government and they liked to talk about it, but in Dean's case, there wasn't much interaction going on. He wasn't rude, but once he had made up his mind, he wasn't interested in spending much time talking about it. He was, says Pelham, "cryptic."

Hogan's new manager said nothing, but to Pelham, she seemed horrified. "If she could have screamed, I think she would have," he says. "Her body language said, 'What have I gotten myself into?'" But everyone who had spent much time in the Dean administration knew what the policy was, and it very seldom was changed.

Dean had no problems with his staff, but he did with the legislature, particularly with the liberal Democrats who then ran the House. He often clashed with Sally Fox, a member of House Appropriations, and Sean Campbell, a budget manager. These legislators were receptive to claims that various elements of government might need more money than they were getting, and some veteran bureaucrats were not above hinting as much when they appeared before an appropriations committee. It was disloyal, of course, but it also was common. Most governors put up with it.

Pelham recalls being in a meeting in the governor's office with Campbell and Dean, wrangling over the budget. "Well, Governor," Campbell said at one point, "even your commissioners are coming in and saying they can't live with this amount."

"Who says so?" Dean wanted to know.

Campbell named a veteran department head.

Dean rose from the white couch, walked to the telephone, called Hogan and told him, "I want you to fire [the department head]." Hogan asked for a little time, but by the end of the legislative session, the man was gone. Pelham was flabbergasted. Dean hated to fire anyone, but he had no sense of humor about the budget.

On another occasion, the commissioner of public safety came in to plead for more overtime money for the state police. Earlier, he had asked for money to hire additional state troopers so they could avoid excessive overtime. But in fact, the state cops love overtime, so the commissioner ended up on the white couch looking for yet more money. Not a chance.

The only real exception to rigid budget discipline was health care, Pelham says. "That is where he really put his pedal to the metal." This did stretch the budget some, but those costs were offset somewhat by increased tobacco taxes.

Overall, general fund expenditures remained under control during Dean's tenure.

Dean kept Ralph Wright's promise to Snelling by moving to end the progressive income tax structure once the deficit had been retired. Even there, however, he went Snelling one better. He cut the income tax rate from 25 percent of the federal rate to 24 percent, which pleased his friends in the business community.

"It was enormously important in the symbolic sense," says Nord Brue of the tax cut. "He was the best of any Democrat. He was a guy you could do business with. If anyone was even thinking of opening a business in Vermont, Howard was on the phone."

This budget discipline, however, raised the question of whether the agencies were getting enough money to do their jobs. The Agency of Natural Resources, for example, was under constant pressure to do better at monitoring development permits. Several other agencies had problems as well.

"I agree they didn't have enough money to do what they were authorized to do," Pelham says. And the normal Democratic appetite for new spending on social programs was harshly suppressed.

Ralph Wright was never tempted to kiss Howard Dean.

HEALTH CARE

One key plank in Howard Dean's presidential platform is his assertion that he provided health care insurance for all of Vermont's children. There is both more and less to that than meets the eye.

In fact, the program known as Dr. Dynasaur, which provides health care benefits to children and pregnant women, was designed and passed into law in 1989 by Gov. Kunin, Dean's predecessor; and though Dean was her lieutenant governor, he had nothing to do with it. Yet he did expand it and, more than that, he for the first time pushed governmental health care coverage out beyond the welfare population to working people who did not qualify for Medicaid. And he was willing to spend serious money on it, in contrast to most other areas of government. Beginning in the early 1980s, Vermont moved to the forefront of the health care reform movement. The principal issues were first, cost containment, and then, as the number of uninsured began to grow, the ability of people to get care. Gov. Snelling set a strong regulatory structure in place for Vermont hospitals, and very nearly succeeded in getting state authority to cap hospital operating budgets, something that existed nowhere in the United States.

The pressure for reform increased during the Kunin administration in the mid- to late-1980s. The legislature established a working group to design a complete restructuring plan for the health care delivery system in the state and, in 1988, the group produced its report. The key elements were tough cost controls, along with a series of devices to ensure health care coverage for every citizen.

Kunin had pledged to deliver universal access to care, but as she began to build her budget in 1988, the economy was sliding into recession. Moreover, it was becoming clear that the cost would be prohibitive: It had started out at about $40 million, but the recession was driving up the number of uninsured and the total cost was moving to the neighborhood of $90 million. So, in 1989, Kunin ordered her staff to find a fallback position.

They found it deep in the big plan that had been developed by the working group: One legislative piece would provide prenatal care for pregnant women who had incomes up to 225 percent of the federal poverty level; the second would provide health care coverage for kids up to age 6. Actually, the most important of these two pieces was the prenatal care, since care in the first trimester is vital to the health of newborns.

Neither piece, however, was very expensive. The program, with an appropriation of $1.5 million, passed on the last day of the 1989 legislative session. The health care bureaucrats hired a public relations firm to get them a name. It was Dr. Dynasaur.

Dr. Dynasaur was a small but important step forward. It took a small bite out of the numbers of uninsured, but it did nothing for cost containment and it did not solve the really knotty problems of health care for the working poor, especially the post 50-year-olds whose bodies were wearing out and who would be in trouble until they got picked up by Medicare at age 65. Hence, it did nothing to ease the pressure for health care reform.

As Vermont entered the 1990s, the reform movement was cresting here and in a handful of other states — Minnesota, Oregon, Florida, Hawaii. Snelling's response was to set up a blue-ribbon commission to design a comprehensive program. All the important health policy players were members. Dean had no role to this point, even though he was lieutenant governor and a physician. Snelling paid no more attention to his views than Kunin had.

Most of the reform proposals at the time contemplated keeping the health care system in the private sector, but otherwise erecting government mechanisms to control costs and provide various subsidies for the uninsured. There was another idea out there, however — a Canadian-style single payer, in which government is the only source of financing. A few members of the Vermont Senate favored this approach — and so, as lieutenant governor, did Howard Dean.

In late February 1991, then–Lt. Gov. Dean testified before the Senate Health and Welfare Committee in favor of a single-payer bill that had been introduced in the Senate. Dean told senators they should pass the bill "in the next two weeks." The committee members were astonished. "I'm totally serious about that," Dean said. "I'm not kidding. . . .

"As you know, I support national health insurance, and one reason is that we have to have universal access," he continued. That single-payer bill didn't pass, but the idea persisted.

In early 1992, after Dean had become governor, the legislature established another group, this time a three-member authority, that was charged with designing two comprehensive health care reform bills: One would be a regulated multi-payer bill and the second, a single-payer bill along the lines of that Senate bill. The authority delivered both plans to the 1994 legislature.

This time, Dean embraced the multi-payer model. It essentially provided for some state financing for the uninsured and additional constraints on costs. The support for it was enormous. There was an informal consensus of the shrewdest players in the Statehouse — committee chairmen, lobbyists and veteran reporters. Without exception, they predicted a major reform bill would pass.

There was also unanimity that it would not be a single-payer bill; Dean would no longer support it. He had had no budget responsibility when he testified in favor of it as lieutenant governor, but he surely did now, and the system would cost hundreds of millions of dollars.

In his memoir, former Speaker Ralph Wright says of this period: "Dean could break out in a rash at the mere mention of the smallest increase in the most obscure tax. To propose raising, by over $700 million, the one tax that had an impact on all working Vermonters, probably brought him to the edge of a stroke."

Speaker of the House Ralph Wright, left, and Howard Dean listen to an address in the early 1990s.
(Times-Argus *Photo by Sandy Macys*)

Legislators in the House dove into the problem of rebuilding the health care delivery system along new lines. Dean, who often seemed indifferent to the staffing of his office since he did most of the heavy lifting himself, in this case put an excellent team in the field. But the real manager of the bill was Wright himself. He convened a special committee of legislators. Over the next three months, all the key players threw themselves into one of the toughest legislative challenges any of them would ever confront.

They failed utterly. The reasons are mind-numbingly complex, but they can be summed up in the idea that every time you tinker with one piece of the current system, it causes unintended changes in another part. It wasn't anybody's fault, really, and it certainly wasn't Dean's. The health care reform movement collapsed everywhere, not just in Vermont, but in other states out front with the issue. The most sensational train wreck was the national effort by Hillary and Bill Clinton, which failed at about the same time.

The Vermont players were devastated by their inability to solve the problem. Dean's top staffers on the issue packed up and left the state. One person who took it especially hard was Wright: He was one of the most politically skilled people to ever serve in the Statehouse, and he wanted this badly. Dean would have claimed the credit, which he should, but this bill would have really been Wright's.

Wright still held out some hope that something might be salvaged by the Senate. That hope didn't last long. On the evening that the effort collapsed in the House, he and Dean happened to be together on a plane heading to a fund-raiser in Washington.

He describes the scene in his memoir:

"'Governor,' I said, 'what are we going to do with the Health Care Plan in the Senate?' I was prepared for a lengthy dialogue carefully outlining an advance to final victory. I didn't have any such plan, but this was the governor's baby, and I had the hope of a child that father would now outline how to get the job done right.

"He barely looked up from his reading and he nonchalantly answered, 'Nothing, it's dead.'

"That's it? It's dead. Two years of grinding and fighting and it's dead? Everything went out of my mind, as the only visual I had was the Governor in a hospital room, pulling another sheet up over a patient's face, and turning to look at the charts on the patient in the next bed. We had little to talk about the rest of the flight. . . .

"I guess this was the one thing I never could understand

about Howard Dean. He always seemed so ready to abandon his cause at the first sign of defeat. Maybe it was his medical training that toughened him to the certain failures that awaited us all. Maybe it was an unwillingness to have any cause at all, at least any cause for which he was willing to risk his political skin.

"Thus, it was a surprise he abandoned health care, the one cause he could have justifiably taken credit for. Even in defeat, he could have held his head high, but to me a lot of the pride and glory was sapped from the whole affair by his willingness not to fight to the very end. He was too quick to run up the white flag. It wasn't just causes he was willing to abandon, he was capable of acting the same with people."

Dean's response to failure was to move to an incremental approach. That summer, he called the state's bureaucrats to a meeting at a children's camp in Waterbury, just outside Montpelier, and gave them a pep talk about finding ways to bite into the problem of the uninsured. He directed the state's bureaucrats to mine the deep recesses of the federal Medicaid regulations to render more and more low-income workers eligible for the program that had been designed for welfare recipients. In this, they were successful; by the turn of the century, 22 percent of the state's population had coverage under Medicaid, more than in any other state.

The administration managed the costs in part by establishing a special health care trust fund that acted as a receiver of money from tobacco taxes. But, as Tom Pelham notes, health insurance eligibility was one of the few places, perhaps the only place, that Dean would slacken his iron grip on state expenditures. He saw the uninsured as a problem, and while he wouldn't fight for a comprehensive solution, which so disappointed Wright, this was a problem he worked to solve. In large measure, he succeeded.

SUCCESS BY SIX

Howard Dean was not only the longest-serving Vermont governor in the post–World War II era, he was one of the most unusual. His administrative style was the product of striking contradictions. He was the straight talker who could also shift positions without a qualm. He was an aggressive problem-solver who was often eerily detached from his own government. He was a ferocious budget manager who could also throw money at something like a commuter rail system that ended in a farm field. He loved the outdoors and would buy as much land as he could for conservation, but he also favored job creation over environmental regulation.

Dean could be hard to predict, because of his quicksilver mind and intuitive style. This attribute was especially evident when he dealt with such major issues as management of the budget and tax policy, health care, civil unions and the environment. But the less portentous issues illustrate his style as well. Government observers in

Gov. Howard Dean talks to Bonnie Johnson-Aten of Montpelier at a public forum on heroin, alcohol and drug abuse.
(Times-Argus *Photo by Stefan Hard*)

Vermont usually cite two highlights among Dean's accomplishments in office: tight budget management of the state's economy, and Success by Six, an effort to link early education programs to social services. The budget part is concrete enough, but it is illuminating that Dean's most striking program is not really a program at all.

Success by Six actually had its origins in Snelling's last administration. It was developed in the summer of 1991 by the head of the state's Human Services Agency, Con Hogan, who continued on in Dean's administration. The idea of the program was to coordinate the human services and education agencies, packaging various children's programs to help kids and thereby making them more effective. Immunization for youngsters, well-baby visits for newborns, testing for lead poisoning, hearing tests, programs to prevent sex abuse, to prevent teen pregnancies and second teen pregnancies, early education efforts — all would work in concert to have more impact.

When the concept was presented to Dean, Hogan recalls, "he almost jumped out the window. He saw the potential to affect whole communities. He was able to package the stuff and make it saleable in the legislature." The cost of the coordination was very low, Hogan says, and Dean always loved that. What struck Hogan most, however, was Dean's enthusiasm for it.

Every Friday, Hogan wrote a brief report to the governor on his agency's activities. He tried always to include some tidbit of data on Success by Six, such as, "This week completed 100 percent immunization in St. Johnsbury."

Then, at Dean's weekly news conference, Hogan would see Dean at the podium with a whole contingent from the affected community: interested citizens, program beneficiaries, bureaucrats from the local social-service agencies and local officials. Dean would have his arm around the kids, and he would be congratulating them about making Success by Six work.

This selling job made the whole thing succeed. The public grew much more aware of the individual programs and their benefits, and the bureaucrats, caught up in a sort of public crusade, seemed to work with greater zeal. Dean, perhaps because of his medical training, demanded measured results, and Hogan and his staff gave them to him: well-baby visits, up from 10 percent of births to 92 percent; sex abuse of children, down 50 percent; teen pregnancies, lowest in the United States; lead levels in the brains of children, down by half; second births to teens, an ominous measure of social dysfunction, down by a third; hearing tests for kids completed by age one and one half years, down from 6.

WELFARE REFORM

A second program that Hogan brought to Dean in the fall of 1991 was welfare reform. This process also had been initiated in the Snelling administration. Dean approved the bill along with a raft of others. "We're going to go for it," Dean told

Hogan. "We're not going to change a word. These are all good, sound, humane changes." For the most part, however, Dean left this effort to Hogan and his senior staff to develop.

The core of the bill was known as workfare, a requirement that welfare recipients get a job after a limited period on the rolls. The job could be in the private sector, but failing that the recipient would have to take a public service job. The Clinton administration was moving in the same direction; both the state and national governments were driven by research showing that workfare could break the chain of welfare dependency across generations. The move to greater independence would be cushioned by several safety nets, including an increase in the cutoff age for the Dr. Dynasaur health program and formulas to allow welfare recipients to keep a larger percentage of their earnings as they started working.

The bill got a mixed reception when it went to the health and welfare committees. On the House side, the panel was dominated by liberals who loved it. On the Senate side, the committee, likewise dominated by liberals, hated it. The bill died in the Senate, without much input from Dean.

It didn't pass in the subsequent session either, but Hogan says Dean stepped into the fray at that point and ordered a special one-day session of the legislature to approve the measure. It was the governor's leadership at this point, Hogan says, that made the bill possible. He had showed little interest in the nuts and bolts, but then his bold personal stroke solved the problem.

EDUCATION FUNDING

The Vermont Supreme Court played an unprecedented role in the fortunes of the Dean administration. The highest-profile case was the one that led to the creation of civil unions — the granting of marriage-like rights to homosexuals — which roiled state government as it had never been roiled before. The court also ordered the governor and the legislature to solve the problem of huge differences in public school spending from town to town, depending on whether the town was rich or poor.

This problem had been festering for decades. Without

action by the high court, it might have festered for decades more. The underlying problem was that since schools were funded largely through local property taxes, wealthy towns — with expensive homes or valuable commercial and industrial property — could spend lots of money on their schools, whereas poorer towns had much less to spend. What made this situation particularly galling was that homeowners in the poor towns paid high property tax rates, while property owners in wealthy towns, many of them very wealthy themselves, paid low rates.

The critical question was how to raise the necessary money, and more specifically, whether to establish a local income tax as part of the financing formula. The income tax question set Dean in opposition to House liberals, who had been working on the matter for several years and who were determined to use a local income tax not only to raise money, but as a device to redress what they considered inequities in school financing generally. They lost. Dean, supported by what at the time was a more conservative Senate, prevailed. The final system of funding depended on increases in various broad-based taxes on corporations, telecommunications and the like, as well as a mechanism that forced wealthy towns to share their property tax revenues with poorer communities.

Fending off an increase in income-based taxes achieved one of Dean's primary objectives — to make the state as attractive as possible to business and industry. There was no way, however, to avoid adding to state taxes, and some Republicans blame Dean for this. However, it is hard to see how this increased burden could have been avoided, given the Supreme Court decision. And critics tend not to give Dean credit for offsetting the total weight of taxation by reducing the local property tax burden.

In any event, the court-driven restructuring of school financing galvanized conservatives, who hated the perceived loss of local control of schools, and some residents of wealthy towns, who resented seeing their local tax dollars go into another community's schools. While not as critical as civil unions, school financing was a factor in the eventual shift of the Vermont House to Republican control.

OTHER INITIATIVES

Dean had an unusual administrative style, and one way in which that was most evident was in transportation. He was fascinated by the subject. Julie Peterson, his chief of staff in the latter part of his tenure, recalls that he would often call the office from his car, inquiring about the status of road construction he passed.

His first major public pronouncement on a transportation issue came in the summer of 1992, after just less than a year in office. The subject was an effort by the state Agency of Transportation to carve back the steep rock walls that lined Interstates 89 and 91 in several locations. The purpose was to improve safety: Drivers who went off the road had only a few feet to recover control or stop.

Some members of the public were outraged, however, at the sight of these soaring rock faces being blown up and skinned sharply back. There were demonstrations. One man climbed one of the walls and said he wouldn't come down until the program was halted.

At his news conference one day, Dean simply exploded about this project. He said he wanted it stopped. "I got sick and tired of looking at it on my way back and forth between Montpelier and Burlington," he told the press.

Dean had said the agency had until the end of 1993 to finish the project, but in July 1993 he just shut it down. "I'm not a safety expert," he said. "If someone gets killed, then it's one someone who didn't have to die. It's very hard to second guess this. But I react the way a Vermonter has to, to this. I don't like it."

What was remarkable about this incident was Dean's apparent detachment from the machinery of his own government. He spoke about it as the ordinary Vermonter might; it also sounded as if the agency would do what it should do or get sent to its room.

Glenn Gershaneck, who served first as Dean's press secretary and then as his secretary of transportation, says the appearance of detachment came from Dean's style, which was to give the agency secretaries something close to full autonomy, but then to hold them accountable publicly. "He had no qualms about disagreeing with activity in the agency," he says.

While Dean was extraordinarily tight with state money, he would occasionally go overboard on a project he liked. An example was the Champlain Flyer, a commuter train from the Burlington waterfront south through the suburbs of South Burlington (population 16,000) and Shelburne (7,000). The southern terminus was a farm field in Charlotte, a town of 3,500 people. This was by far the tiniest mass transit project in the United States. A one-way fare was $1, but ridership was such that revenues were only $100,000 a year, while operating costs were $2.5 million. Government subsidies amounted to roughly 96 percent of the actual cost, which is extremely high but not unprecedented. Supporters of the train argued that ridership might have been higher had a nearby road construction project tied up commuter traffic as had been expected.

Dean's successor pulled the plug on the project in 2003. But it was an example of Dean's willingness to stick with a project he liked, even though quixotic. "He really had a passion for it," Gershaneck says.

When it comes to certain issues, though, Dean has remained fluid.

On the death penalty, for example, he has moved to the right. When he assumed office he opposed capital punishment, but he shifted his ground, saying he supports the death penalty for the killer of a child or police officer or for a terrorist. Some press reports have charged Dean with shifting his views in preparation for running for president.

In fact, however, Dean began to shift as early as 1994. In a news conference in June that year, he said he was still opposed but that he was reconsidering in the case of child murderers. Referring to the slaying of 12-year-old Polly Klaas in California the previous year, Dean said he couldn't think of any redeeming social value in keeping her murderer alive.

Hamilton E. Davis

Gov. Howard Dean completes hiking the 270-mile Long Trail at the Canadian border near East Richford, Vermont, on June 4, 2001. Dean started hiking sections of the Long Trail in September 1992 and covered all of it in 26 different hikes and occasional overnight excursions.

(AP Photo by Mike Riddell)

CHAPTER 6

Green and Not Green

A clear fault line runs down the center of Howard Dean's stewardship of Vermont's environment. On one side is his strong support for the purchase of wild land that might otherwise be subject to development; during his 11 years as governor, the state bought more than 470,000 acres of such land — forest and bog land in the far northeast, parcels encompassing the hiking trails in the Green Mountains, sand plains on the shores of the islands in Lake Champlain.

From his first days in office, putting money into conservation was a high priority for Dean, even when virtually all the rest of state government was on small rations because of his determination to retire the state deficit. The conservation community gives Dean the highest marks for this record.

On the other side of the fault, however, is Dean's record on the regulation of retail and industrial development. His critics charge that his preference for the interests of large business over environmental protection sapped the vitality from the state's regulatory apparatus, especially Act 250, Vermont's historic development-control law, and from regulations pertaining to storm water runoff and water pollution. The result, they say, was unwise large-scale development and degraded water quality, particularly in the northwest part of the state.

Dean's defenders concede he is not much interested in process, but they say his deal-making approach protected the environment more than would strict adherence to the letter of the development-control apparatus. And they criticize some members of the environmental community for not working more closely with the governor to achieve those results.

As for the business community, many of its members have argued for years that the need for jobs and tax revenue should moderate the rigor with which environmental protection laws are applied, and in general they tend to range themselves against the environmentalists. Nevertheless, some business people are also uneasy about weakening the regulatory process; governors, after all, can change, and a different governor could be hostile to development on principle.

In examining these issues, two additional points should be kept in mind.

The first is that while many environmentalists agree that Dean's performance on protection is flawed, they are ambivalent about him now that he is running for president. Their problems with Dean are as nothing compared with their seething dislike for President Bush.

Elizabeth Courtney, the executive director of the Vermont Natural Resources Council, one of the state's leading environmental organizations, feels this conflict acutely. She was badly battered by Dean in the 1990s, but feels better about him now. Chatting in her office about the Dean political phenomenon in early September 2003, Courtney pressed her hands to her temples and said: "I get calls about this all the time, and I watch myself shifting. . . . Here is Howard Dean running for president and he could beat George Bush — wouldn't that be awesome."

The second point to remember is that environmental issues play a big role in Vermont, perhaps more so than in any other state. Concerns about the Vermont landscape are woven into the fabric of life in the Green Mountain State. For one thing, the state is very small, with a population of just 600,000, and is much more rural than most. Burlington, the largest city, has just

40,000 people. The capital, Montpelier, has 8,000. So the countryside, the natural world, looms large indeed. And Vermonters, especially the newcomers who flowed into the state over the past three decades from more urban areas, are generally concerned about protecting, in some cases cosseting, the landscape.

Vermont was the first state to ban billboards on its highways; it was also one of the first to put a deposit on beer and soda bottles; and it has the toughest water-quality and development-control regulations in the country. Only Oregon, with its green belts around Portland, is in the same class in the environmental protection game.

What's interesting is that while much of the muscle behind Vermont's environmental movement is located in an increasingly Democratic electorate, the most striking monuments to environmental protection were put in place by Republicans. Act 250 was designed and pushed through the legislature in 1970 by an otherwise conservative governor, Deane Davis, a native Vermonter, who was appalled by the shoddy nature of second-home developments sprouting in the late 1960s near ski areas.

> There was a consensus, broad and deep, that the state could protect its landscape while effectively managing its economy.

In the 20 years between the landmark law's passage and Howard Dean's becoming governor, Act 250 became an article of faith for Vermont Republicans as well as Democrats. There was a consensus, broad and deep, that the state could protect its landscape while effectively managing its economy. In fact, some scholars in the field posited that Vermont's environmental protection actually helped the economy by making the state an attractive place to visit and do business.

When Howard Dean became governor he therefore faced a high bar on the environment, both in terms of the records of his predecessors and in the expectations of a sophisticated community of environmental advocates. During his long tenure, he more than fulfilled their expectations on land conservation. On other forms of environmental protection, he broke their hearts.

A CHAMPION OF WILD LANDS

Perhaps the most striking conservation effort in Vermont's history was the purchase of the so-called Champion lands, 132,000 acres of wild land lying across the northeast highlands of the state. The late George Aiken, former governor and senator, described this region as the Northeast Kingdom, and for many Vermonters it embodies their heritage: a piedmont of low, forested hills, dotted with ponds and lakes, interspersed here and there by farms eking out a living on the thin soil, icy cold much of the year. The forests have been logged, and logged again, which makes it excellent hunting country; the scrub trees and brush that grow up on clear-cut tracts make excellent feed for deer. Back in the hills are hundreds of what Vermonters call deer camps, cottages and shacks where men, and increasingly women, repair in the fall for the annual hunt. The towns are small; most have just a handful of residents, and one, Lewis, has no residents at all. The people who live in the Northeast Kingdom are generally conservative about land ownership. They care passionately about the right to log and, in the winter, to snowmobile.

In October 1997, the paper manufacturer Champion International Co. announced that it would sell all its holdings in New York, Vermont and New Hampshire, a total of 300,000 acres. In Vermont, the environmental community immediately mobilized to get control of the 132,000 acres in the state and thereby foreclose extensive second-home development. The cost for the purchase would be $26.5 million.

The deal — embraced by Dean — eventually was fashioned by a consortium of environmental groups. The arrangement was complex, but essentially it required that the state kick in $4.5 million toward the total cost and in return it would gain control of a 22,000-acre tract centered on West Mountain in the towns of Lewis and Ferdinand.

The state land would be divided into two sections. The so-called core area was the 12,500-acre parcel around West Mountain itself. This was to be set aside as wild land, with no logging. The owners of the camps in the area would be allowed to keep them for their own lifetimes, plus 20 years, but then the properties, which had been leased from Champion, would revert to state control. Roads through the area would gradually fade into disuse, but people could still use the land to hike, hunt or fish. No snowmobiles or other engine-driven vehicles would be allowed. Over time, the forest canopy would grow more dense and the area would become prime habitat for certain kinds of songbirds and much less suited for game species like ruffed grouse, deer and moose. Fishing, however, would improve: The closed-in canopy would keep water temperatures lower in the streams, making them more hospitable for wild brook trout.

The other half of the state's tract, 9,500 acres, would be managed in a more permissive way, with logging and snowmobiles allowed. This section is envisioned to become ideal game habitat, as clear-cut areas grow up to brush.

This arrangement was a compromise based on what Howard Dean would accept; the environmental community bought into it because the groups needed Dean's support in the legislature to make the deal stick; and the National Rifle Association and the Vermont Federation of Sportsmen's Clubs went along because the area remained opened for hunting.

But the plan was strongly opposed by the camp owners, who organized a group supporting traditional uses to push to keep the whole area open to logging and motorized access; they also wanted perpetual leases on the camps. This group vilified Dean for his support for a core wilderness area, yet he maneuvered with considerable skill to keep enough support from the sportsmen's groups to make it happen.

Some environmentalists thought the state should have set aside the entire 22,000 acres as an ecological reserve. In a fly fishing magazine, for example, Ted Williams, a nationally noted environmental writer, argued that a core area with real biological integrity should be at least 40,000 acres. In fact, however, there was little support for anything that big.

Bob Klein, executive director of the Vermont chapter of The Nature Conservancy, credits Dean for holding the whole Champion deal together, especially the treatment of the West Mountain natural area. "I can't imagine a more sympathetic or supportive person to be in the governor's chair," Klein says. "He really does have a personal interest in this kind of thing and he put his money where his mouth is."

Klein also says this kind of support marked Dean's tenure from the beginning and involved far more than just the Champion lands. The vehicle for state land conservation in Vermont is the Housing and Conservation Board, and Klein notes that Dean always channeled as much money to its fund as he could. He also put in his budget some money to help preserve sections of the Long Trail, the 270-mile hiking path running along the spine of the Green Mountains from the Massachusetts border to Canada. Dean is a hiker and he was known for slipping away from his official duties with his state police driver and hiking sections of the trail. By the time he left office, he had hiked it all.

Dean's normal pattern on land preservation was to work with state senator Dick Mazza, a popular and respected Democrat, who has spent 20 years in the Senate. Mazza would baby-sit the conservation money through the system. In a normal year, Mazza says, Dean would get $300,000 to $500,000 for the Long Trail and $10 million to $12 million for Housing and Conservation. This amounts to serious money in Vermont. Even early in his governorship, when he was trying to retire a deficit, Dean was generous with money for land conservation.

"Howard would call me in a couple of times a week and we would talk about it," Mazza says. "If he thought something was in trouble, he'd say, 'OK, Dick, I think we've got a problem here. . . . Can you help?' He always knew the issues well; he always knew where the pressure was coming from. Howard had his hand on the throttle."

One thing that impressed Mazza over the years was that

Dean kept in touch with him regularly, not just when he needed something. And he was always ready to help his friends when they needed a hand. "It wasn't a one-way street with Howard," Mazza says. "If you needed something, he was right there to help you."

Dean conserved other large blocks of land, including property around Moore's Reservoir on the Connecticut River — much like a lake in the river — on Vermont's border with New Hampshire, and a 600-acre tract along Lake Champlain that eventually became Alburg Dunes State Park. He also aggressively funded recreational projects, such as bike paths. One striking instance of enthusiasm for this kind of thing was his support, in a declining economy, for construction of a bike bridge over the Winooski River, between Burlington and the town to the north. He stayed with this project even when the cost blew up from $1.4 million to $3 million.

This aspect of Dean's environmental record embodied his approach toward the budget. The money he would spend would not require significant additional funds to maintain a program. The expenditures were one-time. If times got bad and money was tight, he could simply spend less. The purchase of the various lands would have little or no effect on the economy, and, of course, it would represent no problem for major em-

> "I can't imagine a more sympathetic or supportive person to be in the governor's chair."
>
> Bob Klein,
> *Executive Director, Vermont Chapter of The Nature Conservancy*

ployers. And the pattern of the purchases fit into Dean's personal inclinations: He had canoed on Moore's Reservoir with his kids, and he used the Burlington bike path all the time. And he loved to hike.

Dean mentioned to Julie Peterson, his chief of staff, one morning that he had hiked 18 miles on the lf;gk the previous day. A hike of even half that distance in the Green Mountains is a challenge. The trails are steep and paved with roots and broken granite. Only the most hard-core trekker achieves such distances on that trail.

Dean considers himself an environmentalist, but he insisted on doing it his own way, finding solutions to problems as they arose and then negotiating toward those ends. This approach worked well on land conservation.

The environmentalists, however, believe that in the area of regulations on development and water pollution his disdain for the processes written into the law, combined with his desire to bring jobs and economic growth to the state, undermined a system that had served well for 20 years. The most notable example occurred early in his time as governor.

A TEST FOR ACT 250

U.S. Route 5 is the old north-south highway along the state's eastern border, a two-lane ribbon running between farms and second-growth woods and passing through the towns on the western bank of the Connecticut River. South of Bellows Falls, by Vermont's standards a medium-size city, the road is almost entirely rural, running through the small towns of Westminster, Putney and Dummerston.

Then, as you round a sweeping curve near Brattleboro, the vista changes abruptly. What catches the eye is the massive chocolate-colored bulk of C&S Wholesale Grocers, a two-story warehouse framed against the mass of Wantastiquet Mountain in New Hampshire. The warehouse is the anchor of a somewhat disorganized industrial area that morphs into strip development running toward the center of the town.

In the early 1990s, C&S Grocers applied for permission to build a second warehouse, a smaller one, in an industrial park on U.S. 5 (the Putney Road), just over a mile from the first warehouse. The company said the second warehouse would require 300 additional employees.

C&S was the linchpin of the economy in southeastern Vermont. It imports food products from all over the world, stores and repackages them, and reships them to supermarkets along the East Coast. The company's revenues in the early

1990s came to $2 billion a year, and the company was one of Vermont's largest private employers. In 2003, *Forbes Magazine* listed C&S as the 14th-largest privately held firm in the United States.

The project was a politician's delight, and Howard Dean was all for it. There were all those jobs, for one thing, and the tax revenues that would flow from them; furthermore, the new building would go into an industrial park well inside the Brattleboro town limits, not sprawling out in some beautiful farm field. Of course, the project would need a permit under Act 250, the state's development-control law.

Act 250 contains 10 criteria against which such projects are tested. These criteria prohibit a project that would create undue air and water pollution, hurt water supplies or school services, or contribute to excessive soil erosion. The criteria require that the project adhere to the town and regional plans and that it limit the effect on traffic volume and safety. This latter expectation spelled trouble for C&S.

The main C&S warehouse was served by large numbers of tractor-trailer trucks that came and went all hours of the day and night. They were all diesel-powered and many of them were refrigerated, which meant the engines couldn't be turned off. The truck traffic was so heavy that often they couldn't get into the plant immediately, so they would park anywhere they could — side roads, parking lots, wherever. A common sight was a brace of semis idling in the parking lot of the Howard Johnson restaurant a half-mile down the road.

Nevertheless, on July 17, 1992, the three-member Environmental Commission for that district issued an Act 250 permit for the project. Two of the three commissioners voted in favor. The chairman dissented, primarily because of the traffic problems.

"The introduction of an average of 310 tractor trailer trips and up to 600 on peak days, introduces an unacceptable risk of accidents, given the serious existing deficiencies on Putney Road," he wrote. As for the aesthetics criterion, he asserted that the truck traffic would be "offensive and shocking," and as for its compliance with the regional plan, he argued that Putney Road already had a "poor" rating by the state transportation agency. In addition, he said, the regional plan specifies that "development, which generates unsafe traffic conditions, especially on highways with low sufficiency ratings . . . should be avoided."

The dissent was the first shot in what would be a tremendous battle over the C&S application, a battle that would have implications for Act 250 itself and, in fact, for environmental regulation over the following decade.

The district commission decision began to inspire serious local resistance. One group of opponents, many of them from the towns north of Brattleboro, formed the Windham [County] Citizens for Responsible Growth. They appealed the district commission's decision to the state Environmental Board.

The Environmental Board is a nine-member body appointed by the governor; the chairman is a state employee; the other members are citizen volunteers who get a per diem for attending meetings. This type of citizen-based structure is common in Vermont. The Environmental Board and its twin, the Water Resources Board, act as appeals courts in the reg-

Gov. Howard Dean skis in a race against other New England governors at the Killington ski area in Vermont in 1993.
(Rutland Herald *Photo by Vyto Starinskas*)

ulatory system. Witnesses are sworn in, and many rules of court procedure are followed. The only appeal of their decisions is to the Vermont Supreme Court.

Through the spring of 1993, the Environmental Board held hearings on the C&S application. The sessions were packed, and opponents of the project were emotional. There were extensive discussions about traffic. The company's consultant said flow might actually improve with the extra trucks, as long as some traffic signals were added. The opponents, however, steadily picked the company's case apart. Two local residents rented a room in a motel across the street from the main warehouse and counted the number of trucks going in and out. They came up with a number considerably higher than the one the company had calculated.

The opponents also introduced evidence about the inadequacies of Putney Road, which was not only a narrow two lanes, but which was lined south of the existing warehouse with stores, restaurants and small businesses of all kinds, their entrances in some places only 50 or so feet apart. Yet another difficulty showed up at the spot where an exit from Interstate 91 met Putney Road. At certain times of the day, traffic was already backing up onto the highway itself.

On June 22, 1993, the Environmental Board issued its decision, upholding the permit but restricting the number of trucks that could be loaded onto Putney Road. It left the total daily number of trucks at 600, but it set limits for the 8 a.m. to 9 a.m. rush hour, as well as the 12 to 6 p.m. window. It also restricted the numbers of trucks that could use Route 9 West out of Brattleboro.

The opponents were not entirely pleased, but the company was outraged. "These conditions . . . would make it impossible for C&S Grocers to operate successfully," its attorney wrote. The company asked the board to reconsider.

Howard Dean was furious about the decision, and he was not going to stand for it. In mid-July, he blistered the board in harsh, even personal terms. The board should have taken into account the 300 jobs the project would bring into the state, he said. "We are interested in injecting . . . some common sense into the process," Dean said at his weekly news conference. "If this was out in a farmer's field someplace I could understand it, but this is an industrial park zoned for this sort of thing." In a letter to the local newspaper soon afterward, he said it was "time for reason to rule in regard to the permit process."

This broadside was unprecedented by a governor when dealing with a quasi-judicial process, and it surprised everyone, even some of the lawyers who represented developers in such cases. Dean was not only stepping directly into what is supposed to be a deliberative process based on fact finding and evidence, but in putting the matter in personal terms — the board members, he was clearly saying, simply were unreasonable — he was undermining the whole system. For while he appoints the chairperson and he or she reports to him, the Environmental Board is meant to be independent.

The environmental groups that were involved in the case wrote to the governor, objecting to his comments. They argued that his intervention "threatens to undermine the integrity and independence of the Act 250 process. It encourages the public to believe that politics, not law, is what matters in the protection of the environment . . ." The most important impact of Dean's statements, however, was on the board itself.

"We were shocked," says Elizabeth Courtney, who was chairwoman of the board. "The board was shocked. We realized that since the beginning of Act 250, no governor had responded in any way publicly to a decision." Moreover, the decision was based on a huge body of evidence that seemed overwhelming to the board members — that this case wasn't even a close call.

What made Dean's position particularly perplexing was that there was no provision in Act 250 to trade off economic benefits such as jobs and tax revenues for environmental damage. The underlying premise of the law was that the damage from development had to be limited, and if it couldn't be contained, the board must not issue a permit.

Courtney and the other board members asked for a meeting with the governor and got it, but from their standpoint it wasn't very satisfactory. Dean listened to their arguments about the effects of politicizing the board, but apparently he wasn't moved. "He didn't feel he had overstepped his bounds in any way," Courtney says.

Dean soon confirmed this judgment a short time later when

he was quoted in the *Burlington Free Press* as saying, "I have to be a little careful in my public comments because it is a quasi-judicial board." But he continued to argue that C&S was a major employer and that the project was to be in an area zoned for industrial use.

Shortly after this flurry, the board agreed to reconsider its decision. Its chief counsel at the time, Stephanie Kaplan, said the reason was that the Agency of Natural Resources, which had declined to participate in the case to that point, wanted to testify on some of the permit conditions that fell under its purview. Still, the reconsideration, coming in the immediate wake of the governor's action, was less than reassuring to environmentalists, not to mention the suspicion that the ANR was being brought in not on neutral grounds but with orders to support C&S.

On September 22, 1993, the board issued an amended decision, easing the truck limitations. It allowed 600 truck trips to the new facility a day, with some reductions in constraints on the number that could move in and out during high-traffic periods.

This was not enough for C&S. It decided to build the new facility in Hatfield, Massachusetts, about 50 miles south on Interstate 91. But that was not the end of the story.

THE ENVIRONMENTAL BOARD IN HIS SIGHTS

Dean's attack on the C&S decision, his harsh tone and the suggestion that the board was unreasonable came at a time of growing pressure from Republicans — who then, in 1994, controlled the Senate — to modify the whole Act 250 process. They saw the application of the law as unfair constraint on business and development. And they were gunning for the Environmental Board.

When the legislature opened, the Republicans had a decision that eclipsed anything they had seen before — the C&S case. They also had before them the names of five members of the board whose terms were about to expire. Dean, though unhappy with the board's decision, resubmitted the names of all five, and among them was chairwoman Elizabeth Courtney.

Courtney was a landscape architect and a Democrat who had been appointed to the board by Gov. Madeleine Kunin in 1987. When Richard Snelling took office in 1991, he named Courtney chairwoman. Courtney did not know Snelling at the time, but she had had developers as clients in her architecture practice, and Snelling told her he thought she could strike a balance between the needs of the developers and the law.

Snelling was sensitive to the complaints of the business community that citizen access to the process could slow it to a crawl, and he wasn't bashful about making these views known to Courtney. At one of their early meetings in his office, he was lunching on Cheese Nips, and he was pounding the desk so hard that the crackers were flying out of the box.

"We had some back and forth," Courtney says of this session. "But what I understood was that while he was a pragmatic businessman, he wanted to find the balance and do right by the environment . . . and he never weighed in on the board's decisions. He did not let us know, either directly or indirectly, whether he agreed. He understood his role was to have input on issues not related to [specific cases]."

On the day that Snelling died and Dean took over, Courtney was at the meeting of the extended cabinet. She had expected that Dean would inform them all that he would be installing his own people as soon as he could. But that didn't happen. Dean told them instead that he wanted them to continue as they had been, for the most part. The political climate soon changed for Courtney, however.

A few weeks later she had her own private meeting in Dean's office. Courtney told the governor what was on the board's agenda, but she says she immediately got the impression he wasn't very interested. He told her he wanted her to keep the machinery moving; that he didn't want development unnecessarily delayed. He said he respected Snelling's positions and that he wanted to continue in the same vein. What Dean did not understand, she says, was that Snelling was determined to find a balance, not simply remove impediments to development.

"I remember [thinking] as I was leaving and the door

clicked shut: He's a doctor. I felt a little like a nurse coming out of a consultation with the doctor. The information I gave him was taken with a grain of salt because he was the doctor. He wasn't looking for information, he was looking to inform me."

The Republicans in the Senate seized on the governor's comments about the C&S case and rejected every board member. Dean publicly said he supported all his nominees, but in environmental circles there was considerable suspicion about how committed he was. The full Senate eventually confirmed two of the five, but among the three it rejected was Courtney. She says Dean told her then that he would like to send her name back a second time, but that he didn't want to send the others back. She refused on principle. Dean relented and sent all three back to the Senate, but all three were again rejected.

> "I remember [thinking] as I was leaving and the door clicked shut: He's a doctor. I felt a little like a nurse coming out of a consultation with the doctor."
>
> *Elizabeth Courtney,*
> *Former Chairwoman,*
> *Vermont Environmental Board*

Dean could have continued to resubmit the names and insist they be accepted, and much of the environmental community thought he should. But he gave up. Ralph Wright, for one, never forgave Dean for this. Just as on the health care bill, Wright says in his memoir, Dean was too quick to give up. "Another sheet was drawn over the bodies of three dedicated and long-serving public servants," wrote the former House speaker. "I don't think I've ever been more disappointed than I was at that moment."

Dean then offered Courtney a job in the Agency of Natural Resources, but she turned it down and went off to graduate school. Later she joined the Vermont Natural Resources Council as executive director, where she still serves in 2003.

Pat Parenteau, who served in several roles in Vermont government and went on to teach environmental law at Vermont Law School, is completely scornful. "It was all Howard Dean," he says of the Environmental Board experience. "He put a target on every one of them."

The C&S Grocers case was just one set of circumstances, but its importance extended well beyond Brattleboro, and the trends set in motion there continue to resonate in Vermont's physical environment and in its politics. Huge development projects moved on line in the 1990s, especially in Chittenden County, where Wal-Mart and Home Depot were building bigbox stores in the suburbs of Burlington. The ski areas were expanding too, not only in second-home real estate ventures, but in new snowmaking capability, which involved pumping water from rivers and streams and running it through giant nozzles that turned it to snow and blew it onto the slopes. Environmentalists argued that reducing the water levels in rivers and upland streams damaged habitat for trout and other species.

And as Dean's tenure was drawing to a close, Husky, a Canadian plastics manufacturer, built a huge plant in Milton, a few miles north of Burlington, a project that drew almost no opposition. That delighted the development and business communities but signaled to the environmental community the final hollowing-out of Act 250 — a process that had begun six years earlier with the C&S Grocers case.

Trouble in the Water

While Act 250 has been the centerpiece of the Vermont regulatory apparatus, the state's water quality laws, backed by federal statutes, are almost equally important. Moreover, they are tightly linked. The effect on water quality is a criterion within Act 250, and virtually any development will, at a minimum, cause some degradation of water quality in nearby lakes and streams.

The bureaucratic process for protecting water quality is different from the Act 250 process. The initial permits for water quality are issued by the Agency of Natural Resources, whose staff works directly for the governor, whereas Act 250 permits are issued by the more independent district environmental commissions. The appeal processes, however, are parallel. Regular development appeals go to the Environmental Board; appeals for water permits go to the Water Resources Board.

The most difficult water quality issues have arisen in Chittenden County on Lake Champlain. The county has a population of about 148,000, including Burlington, and is the only really metropolitan area in the state. The first arc of suburbs is densely populated, and the second arc is rapidly getting that way. Development pressures have been steadily growing for three decades. In the 1950s, there were dairy farms within the city of Burlington. Now they are disappearing from the whole county.

One of the epicenters for development is the town of Williston, which lies in the second arc of suburbs but has its own interchange on the highway. A huge commercial area has grown up near the interchange, providing a home for a full complement of big-box retailers, as well as dozens of lesser establishments. People who hate it see it as New Jersey North, but it has been very successful financially.

One problem that comes with such development, however, is storm water runoff. Rain and snow sluice across roads and parking lots, picking up a toxic melange of pollutants — pathogens, heavy metals, oil and gasoline residues. These flow into the rivers and streams, polluting them and then contributing that pollution to Lake Champlain.

The streams that drain the Chittenden County watershed have been deemed "impaired," which means they don't meet either the minimum state or federal standards. And both state and federal law prohibits development that contributes pollutants to an already impaired stream. Given that current technology can capture only 80 percent of pollutants in storm water, these laws present a formidable barrier to development — at least in theory.

While the technical and legal details of this situation can make the eyes glaze over, the fact is that the Agency of Natural Resources had no easy solution to this problem. It could adhere to the law and reject development applications, or it could issue the permits anyway and simply hope for the best. The latter is the course it took. The device the agency used is something called a watershed improvement plan (WIP), which said in essence that the applicant could build a project as long as there was some plan in place that could show enough improvement in water quality to meet the standards within five years.

The ANR issued dozens of these WIPs, but the fact was that water quality was getting worse, not better. Furthermore, the agency simply gave up on monitoring permits that were coming up for renewal. In the late 1990s, environmental groups in the state, including the Vermont Natural Resources Council and the Conservation Law Foundation, had had enough and began appealing the agency permits to the Water Resources Board.

> Environmentalists charge that Howard Dean, by keeping the Agency of Natural Resources budget increases to a minimum, effectively precluded the agency from carrying out its responsibilities.

It didn't help the ANR's case that the agency had to concede it didn't have enough people or money to get the job done.

Six months after Dean left office the board ruled that the ANR could no longer issue permits based on watershed improvement plans, because the agency couldn't be sure the plans would achieve the minimum water quality standards within five years, or indeed within any definite period.

Dean's successor as governor, James Douglas, a Republican who favored relaxing the environmental permit process, was unhappy with the Water Resources Board's decision. But when Douglas decided against appealing to the Supreme Court, it became clear that there simply was no straight-face defense of the agency performance under the Dean administration.

Environmentalists charge that Dean, by keeping the ANR's budget increases to a minimum, effectively precluded the agency from carrying out its responsibilities.

Perhaps even more important than that, however, was that the opponents of Act 250 began to use the agency's failures at enforcement to attack the law itself, which drove some environmentalists to distraction. One of them is Bill Bartlett, who retired after 25 years as executive officer of the Water Resources Board. In a series of op-ed articles in the spring of 2003, he railed against this proposition. "Whatever its faults," he wrote, "Vermont's environmental regulatory process has not created a problem by making Vermont's rivers and streams overly pristine or Lake Champlain too clean." The real problem, he argued, "is that ANR is not doing its job and as a result the backlog of unaddressed problems is growing."

"ANR's failure over a long period of time to properly regulate storm water discharges . . . has left a legacy of expired and unenforced discharge permits, impaired waters, regulatory uncertainty and litigation. . . . ANR has not been given the resources to adequately do its job and too often the scientifically sound recommendations by ANR technical staff are overruled in final permit decisions by political appointees."

BOARD APPOINTMENTS

Beyond the direct pressure a Vermont governor can bring to bear, he or she exerts influence through appointments to bodies such as the district environmental commissions and the Environmental and Water Resources Boards. Equally important is the caliber of the leadership he or she installs at the Agency of Natural Resources.

Since the advent of the environmental laws in the 1970s, Democratic and Republican governors alike have filled the positions in a bipartisan way: taking people who are respected locally and are interested enough in the issues to invest unpaid time. While it is hard to prove — and in any event people in Vermont are loath to discuss the matter because they do not wish to impugn their neighbors — Dean's environmental critics say he moved away from that approach. In his nominations to the various citizen bodies and with some of his appointments to the ANR, Dean seems to have looked to people who wouldn't oppose his philosophy, who wouldn't demand tiresome scientific data and who wouldn't mind working for a governor who might inject himself in cases.

Stephanie Kaplan, the attorney at the Environmental Board, who lost her job during the renomination battle, is vehement about Dean's performance in this regard. She says flatly that Dean eviscerated the protection system. "It is now impossible to have a fair hearing if you oppose a development," she says. "And Howard Dean is responsible . . .

"The worst thing he did was make horrible appointments to the district commissions and to the Environmental Board. He only appointed people who were interested in power or who were very adamantly pro-development. He said we need a hard-nosed businessperson there. When he appointed people, he told them, 'Don't obstruct business.' Even if we get a good governor, it will take years to overcome what he did."

"OPERATION BIG DOG"

The culmination of the hollowing-out of the Act 250 process appeared to come with a development project that began in the mid-1990s. A Canadian company, Husky Injection Moldings Ltd., began to search for a site for a new plant in the eastern United States. One site it considered was a 700-acre farm bordering Arrowhead Lake in Milton, a working-class town just north of Burlington. Howard Dean's administration went all out to attract the company. It set up a system to coordinate the effort within the administration and to link it to critical elements outside state government, such as the Chittenden County Regional Planning Commission and Milton town officials. Administration officials kept it secret and called it "Operation Big Dog."

From an economic perspective, Husky would confer huge benefits on the area. The complex there would be large, some 20 buildings holding about 2,000 workers. And they would be well-paid workers by Vermont standards; the average salary would be $45,000. Husky would resemble a small IBM, whose plant outside Burlington transformed the entire Vermont economy four decades earlier. Finally, Husky had a reputation in Canada as a company with a strong environmental ethic.

The Dean administration effort ran like a military campaign. The project went counter to both the regional plan and Milton zoning, but both of those were changed quickly. The town agreed to bring water and sewer service to the site at a cost of $750,000, even though there were industrial parks with space available both north and south of the farmland. Perhaps the state's most striking offer to the company was to not only permit, but to pay for, a bridge over Arrowhead Lake (not yet built) to enable employees to drive directly to the nearest north-south road.

> "It is now impossible to have a fair hearing if you oppose a development, and Howard Dean is responsible."
>
> Stephanie Kaplan,
> Former Attorney for the
> Vermont Environmental Board

In March 1997, the Husky application went to the district environmental commission. Projects that size usually received a real workout under Act 250; hearings can last for weeks or even months. Husky sailed through in just a few days.

Ironically, in the C&S case, Dean had said he could understand opposition if the project were "out in a farm field somewhere," but in the Husky case, out in a farm field was exactly where it was. The company, however, wanted the open fields and the views, and that was that.

"When I saw that lake, I just fell in love with it," said Robert Schad, the company president.

PRO AND CON

The most uncompromising brief against Howard Dean's record in the protection of Vermont's environment comes from Pat Parenteau, the lawyer on the faculty of Vermont Law School. Parenteau was serving as an enforcement official in the Boston office of the federal Environmental Protection Agency when he was recruited by Gov. Kunin in 1987 to improve Vermont's enforcement regime. Parenteau was described at the time as a man who would take no prisoners in carrying out this writ, and he still hasn't taken a prisoner.

"The big question with Dean is that he was so popular, he had so much power, so much control over legislation, and he really didn't use it," he says. "He squandered so many opportunities to improve water quality. He really did nothing to help Lake Champlain. . . .

> One area where the Dean approach clearly achieved a positive result was on development and snowmaking issues in the ski industry.

"He built great credibility with the business community, because he gave them everything they wanted. He doesn't like lawyers; he doesn't understand process. I think he wrote off the whole management of environmental problems. He completely undercut the Environmental Board.

"He completely polarized the environmental and business communities. His rhetoric was incendiary on behalf of the business community on these kinds of regulatory issues. If he didn't like a decision, he'd pop off."

The most detailed defense of the Dean environmental record comes from David Rocchio, a lawyer who went to work for Dean as deputy counsel in 1997 and soon moved to general counsel. Rocchio was more than just a legal counsel, however; he managed the Dean agenda inside and outside the legislature in half a dozen policy areas.

He cites a long list of environmental accomplishments by the administration: efforts to limit sprawl by encouraging development in downtowns, efforts to prohibit residential development on hilltops, to support controls on auto emissions, to constrain logging practices so as to cut pollution along riverbanks, to close landfills and to finance construction of environmentally safe manure pits on farms to reduce runoff into rivers.

To aid in the management of the regulatory process, Rocchio says, Dean established a development cabinet, a device for coordinating the input of the agencies overseeing natural resources, commerce, transportation, agriculture and public service into development cases.

One area where the Dean approach clearly achieved a positive result was on development and snowmaking issues in the ski industry. The governor and his staff brokered several deals involving land swaps between the state and ski areas that led to protection of undeveloped mountain land. The state kept the high areas wild, and the ski areas got lower-lying tracts for expansion near their base lodges.

Under the leadership of Chuck Clarke, the natural resources secretary in the mid-1990s, the administration and the ski areas also reached an agreement on snowmaking: The resorts would keep streams flowing at their median February level and in return would get the permits they needed. The ski areas made up for the lost water by building storage ponds. The ski industry and the environmental community credit Dean and Clarke with settling an issue that had festered for a decade.

In all of this, however, Rocchio acknowledges that Dean was constantly trying to balance the economic benefits from various projects; and in a case like Husky, he says simply that the economic benefits of locating the project in farmland outweighed some of the other considerations.

"Howard Dean is not a process person," Rocchio says. "He is a doctor. He was always focused on what, in his opinion, was the best thing for the state. He was for bringing as much of the disagreement to the front as possible and then getting it fixed. He wanted to get results through collaboration.

"If you measure all the environmental achievements in water quality, solid waste, non-point source pollution, if you analyze how much environmental good he did as a governor, that sum is much greater than the approach of others who might be more aggressive."

THE DEAN APPROACH

There is a critical disconnect between the approach advocated by Rocchio and that of some environmentalists. Dean disliked formal processes, including those in Act 250 and the water quality regulations, that are encoded in state law. He preferred to drive straight toward whatever result he wanted, whether it was a factory in a farm field or clearance for a ski area to build second homes or make artificial snow. So he would tilt his bureaucrats toward that goal as much as possible and then strike deals with whatever opponents showed up — land swaps, for example, or customized agreements, like the snowmaking arrangements, between the important players.

Environmentalists object to this on the grounds that it politicizes decision-making. Act 250 and other such statutes are designed by the legislature to protect everyone's rights, while achieving some objective — say, improving water quality. They attempt to strike a balance between competing claims, whether they involve the capacity of streams to absorb pollution, or a road network to absorb traffic. They may be slower and less convenient than customized deals between insiders, but they are the way that government normally does business. It is certainly how state government has done business in Vermont under both Democratic and Republican governors.

The difficulty in the Dean approach becomes more apparent when a given deal comes apart. That is what happened with the water quality regulations in the summer of 2003. Once the Water Resources Board had to rule on the law, the informal system that had been in place for several years simply vanished, and it pretty much shut down development in Chittenden County. And there was no apparent answer except a return to the legislature.

Hence the disconnect and hence also the dilemma over Howard Dean's legacy on environmental regulation.

The most nuanced view of this question by an environmentalist is held by Elizabeth Courtney, who by the summer of 2003, with President Bush up for re-election, had mellowed on Dean.

While acknowledging the damage from the C&S and storm water runoff cases, she says she thinks Dean never really understood the damage he was doing to the regulatory system. And she believes he was shifting his posture toward the end of his tenure. For example, she says that in the 2002 session of the legislature, Dean was instrumental in bringing the business and environmental communities together to pass legislation aimed at breaking the impasse on the water quality permits. "I really think he made a positive contribution at the end of his term," she says.

In the fall of 2003, preparing for the coming political and legislative year, Courtney had two major goals. For her organization, VNRC, the goal is to restore the vitality to Act 250, drained away during the Dean administration. The second goal, purely personal, was to do whatever she could to get Howard Dean elected president.

GOVERNOR WITH A SMALL "G"

Say this about Howard Dean: He is his own man.

He tends to think through problems himself, rather than work them out in consultation with others. According to Julie Peterson, one of his closest longtime aides, Dean gets many of his ideas at home at night or while riding in his car.

"He would come into the office and say, 'I was thinking of this last night. Let me try it out on you,'" she says. He moved very quickly, sometimes too quickly, according to Peterson. But she and all his staff had tremendous confidence in his intellectual capacity.

Dean often spoke on an issue before receiving advice from his staff. It was common, Peterson says, for Dean's press secretary to get a call from a reporter asking about some comment by Dean that no one in the governor's office knew he had made. Shortly thereafter, Peterson would get a call from, say, Bennington, at the other end of the state, and it would be Dean saying, "You better get ready. I just said this. . . ."

But he was never overwhelmed, never at a loss.

In the office, Peterson says, Dean would be "striding down

the hall followed by 19 people with clipboards, and . . . he'd look at us as if to say, 'What are you all doing here?' He was definitely the leader of the pack."

Dean would listen politely to opposing points of view when the conversation involved people he cared about, but he could be testy and confrontational when challenged on policy by people he didn't know.

He had a reputation for being impulsive and occasionally arrogant.

His staff and his small cadre of friends, however, saw him differently. They liked him enormously, and they were extremely loyal to him. Peterson emphasizes how respectful Dean was to all his staff. This was in some contrast to Gov. Snelling, for example, whose staff likened him to a drill sergeant.

Dean does not drink alcohol or coffee, so the normal social lubricants are foreign to him. He and his staff developed a tradition of getting together over birthdays; there would be one almost every month and they would celebrate it in the office, with Dean sitting around like one of the gang. He would often give personal advice to his staff members, based on his and his wife's early life. But these were not social friendships; his family was very much a private matter.

Dean impressed some of the people who observed him over the years as a man uninterested in the personal aspects of power. He obviously loved being governor, but he didn't seem to be surrounded by any aura. His predecessors, Snelling and Kunin, had a certain presence; they projected power. They were governors with a capital "G." Some of the people who knew Dean best saw him as a governor with a small "g." He was aggressively insistent on his own views, but otherwise he seemed to think of himself as just an ordinary guy.

It was not just political insiders who saw him that way. During Dean's terms in office, his children, Anne and Paul, attended Burlington High School. In their capacity as parents, Dean and his wife, Judy, were around the school a lot, attending parents' nights and other functions. Other kids at school saw

Howard Dean simply as a parent — pleasant, friendly, interested, but in no way exalted.

One reporter who watched Dean over his entire tenure believes his style grows out of a truly serene self-confidence. Dean seemed to her not to need the kind of deference, indeed adulation, that is commonly sought by politicians. He's bright, successful, he grew up rich in a loving family, and he seemed totally secure about who he is.

This unusual personal and political style may lie at the root of Dean's performance on the C&S Grocers case and, indeed, in the whole area of environmental regulation. Dean seemed simply irresponsible in the harsh nature of his criticism not only of the Environmental Board decision, but of the board itself. He said board members were not only wrong, but perversely wrong; they didn't have any common sense. This diatribe was seen, even by some who welcomed the outcome, as simply over the top for a governor dealing with a quasi-judicial body.

Gov. Howard Dean launches a sailboat into Lake Champlain near his Burlington home in 1999. Dean and his son sailed the 120-mile length of the lake in a Sunfish sailboat.
(Times-Argus *Photo by Jeb Wallace-Brodeur*)

There are two ways to look at that. One is to charge that Dean was subservient to the big developers who, in the environmentalist view, have despoiled the Vermont landscape. Pat Parenteau can be found in this corner. Another, however, is to take Elizabeth Courtney's experience at face value and see Dean as a man who never quite grasped the idea that he was something other than a normal guy. He was smarter than most, of course, and with an unusual job, but otherwise he seems to have considered himself an ordinary guy who could say pretty much whatever crossed his mind without getting too wrought up over it. It does not seem to have occurred to him that people expect a governor to act like a governor and that when he acts like just another citizen it can be difficult for all to deal with.

Vermont is so small that the tensions and contradictions of the Dean personality can play themselves out within families. Bill Bartlett, for example, spent his entire career as the executive director of the Water Resources Board; he lives with a more or less chronic, simmering anger about how Dean dealt with not only water quality, but the environment in general. During the last decade, however, his wife, state senator Susan Bartlett, a Democrat, has played a key role in the Senate leadership, and she is supporting Dean in his presidential bid.

It is not that Susan Bartlett disagrees with her husband or that she sees Dean through rose-colored glasses. When asked about him, she uses the metaphor that has become common currency among people trying to understand Dean. He is the doctor, she says. You are the nurse. He will make the diagnosis and lay out the treatment. Your job is to carry out his instructions. This is often not the most effective way to deal with powerful independent players like Sen. Bartlett. So why is she bending all of her considerable energies and talents to getting Dean elected president?

"You have to consider the whole package," she says. "If you look at a broad range of policy, you can always find something that the person is a dismal failure at. I'll buy the whole package. . . .

"You can disagree with Howard. You can say, 'Howard, here's why I think you're wrong about, say, water for ski areas.' He'll listen, then he'll say, 'OK' [in a flat voice], and you'll think, this rock isn't moving.

"But he doesn't stay angry, he doesn't hold grudges. It doesn't mean you can't have a fine relationship on issues that you do agree on. And not everyone in power acts that way. Also, once you work with Howard, you'll have a relationship with him. He will stick with you; he will care about you as a person.

Even if he says, 'That's the stupidest goddamn thing I ever heard,' if you had an accident, Howard would be right there for you. That's what's different."

Bartlett believes it is Dean's unusual personal style that explains his aggressive attitude on the stump in the presidential campaign. "What drives him," she says, "are his family and his kids and having them in a safe community that they can feel good about. What I think he learned in his travels around the country is that the country is not like Vermont. The schools, the communities — the rest of the country used to have that and now it doesn't anymore, and that has really pissed him off.

"That's why he's so angry, because he thinks the country deserves that and he's determined to make it happen. And look at the way people are responding. He says we have a right to this. People want to believe it's possible for things to be good if they work at it. That's what Howard's about."

Hamilton E. Davis

Gov. Howard Dean holds a news
conference at the Statehouse after
signing the civil unions bill on April 26, 2000.
(Times-Argus *Photo by Jeb Wallace-Brodeur*)

CHAPTER 7

Charting a Course for Civil Unions

Fridays were anxious days in Gov. Howard Dean's office in the fall of 1999. Those were the days the state's Supreme Court traditionally issued its decisions, and Dean's staff was bracing for the court to hand down a whopper.

A year earlier, the court had heard arguments in a case filed by three same-sex couples who were suing the state for the right to marry, and the decision was expected any week. Whether the court accepted or rejected gay marriage, the governor faced having to do what he had assiduously avoided while the case was pending: say what he thought about gay marriage.

"Our staff would try to get some sense from the court: 'Will it be this week?' Because if he could have gotten an early look at the decision, it would have given him time to figure out what the right words for him would be," recalls Susan Allen, Dean's press secretary when he was governor. "But they were so tight with this one. No one was leaking anything."

When the court failed to act on Friday, December 17, Dean's aides figured they had a reprieve of at least another week, maybe more with Christmas and New Year's looming. Maybe, with the start of a new legislative session little more than two weeks away, the court would delay its ruling until spring. But shortly after Dean's staff returned to work on

Monday, Dec. 20, the telephone rang in the governor's office. A court official was on the line. The court had reached a decision, and it had been posted on its Web site. Allen hurried down the hallway to her computer to download the 45-page decision. What she read amazed her.

Several of Dean's other aides joined Allen in her office, which looked out on the gold dome of the nearby Statehouse. They conferred briefly and telephoned the governor.

They reached him in Burlington, where he was interviewing candidates for a top state education position. Janet Ancel, the governor's legal counsel, summarized the ruling for the governor, trying to interpret what it would mean for the state.

Essentially, she informed Dean, neither side had won. The court had not granted same-sex couples the right to a state-sanctioned marriage, as the couples had wanted; nor had it rejected gay marriage, as the state had sought. Instead, the justices had decided that under the Vermont Constitution gays and lesbians must be treated the same as heterosexuals. That meant same-sex couples deserved all the rights and responsibilities associated with marriage under state law, though not necessarily the right actually to marry. This equality could be attained, the court said, either by rewriting the state's marriage statutes to include homosexuals or by creating a separate institution for same-sex couples that paralleled marriage. The justices said the job of finding the proper solution was best left to the legislature and the political process — not the judiciary.

> "When you're talking with Howard Dean, you get a lot done in a little bit of time."
>
> *Janet Ancel,*
> *Dean's Former Legal Counsel*

The court couldn't have made life much more difficult for Howard Dean. If it had ruled definitively, yea or nay, on gay marriage, as most observers assumed it would, then Dean could have simply said: The court has spoken. He could have declared his opinion on the issue to be irrelevant. Instead, the ruling had kept the issue alive, forcing the governor to take a position on gay marriage.

Dean had a reputation for making decisions quickly, sometimes impulsively. His response to this, the Baker decision, was no different. Dean knew the ruling would be controversial, so he called a midday news conference at the state Health Department building in Burlington to address the issue.

Ancel, her mind racing, jumped into her silver Honda Civic to make the 40-minute drive from Montpelier to Burlington. Several other staffers caught a ride with her. As she whisked north on Interstate 89, Ancel cursed herself for offering to drive. She needed the time to review the decision — she would have to give the governor a more detailed briefing before he spoke to the media. Instead, she asked a colleague to read it aloud as she drove.

Once she arrived at the Health Department office, Ancel spoke for a moment with Dean. "It was a conversation on the fly," Ancel remembers. It might have been 20 minutes. "When you're talking with Howard Dean, you get a lot done in a little bit of time, so it might have been just five minutes. He's a doctor. When there's something to deal with, he is focused and then moves on."

In the weeks leading up to the ruling, Ancel and Dean had discussed different ways the court might rule and how the governor should respond. "But not this one," she says. "We didn't think of it." They had foreseen that the court might leave the issue to the legislature. If it did so, however, they thought the court would say the Vermont Constitution permitted, but did not require, that same-sex couples be granted the same rights as heterosexual couples. In that scenario, the legislature could decide whether to grant those rights to gays and lesbians. But the court had gone further by ruling that the legislature was constitutionally required to act.

Despite the surprising turn the ruling had taken, Dean decided quickly what to say. Down the hall, members of the Vermont press waited for the governor in the department's modern boardroom. Sunlight streamed through the windows overlooking a bus station and the Cathedral of the Immaculate Conception.

Then Dean strode into the room, and the tapes began to roll.

"COMMON HUMANITY"

Howard Dean was in a bind because Stan Baker wanted to get hitched.

Baker's first marriage had lasted 21 years. Now Baker, the outpatient director for a mental health agency, wanted to get married again, this time to the partner he'd been with for four years. The trouble was his partner was a man. When they applied for a marriage license from their town clerk, their application was rejected. It was illegal under state law.

So Baker and his partner joined two lesbian couples, who had also been denied licenses, and sued the state for the right to marry. Their lawyers were Beth Robinson and Susan Murray, who had helped found the Vermont Freedom to Marry Task Force, an organization fighting for equal rights for gays and lesbians. Even before the case was filed, task force members had launched a public information campaign, setting up booths at county fairs, talking to Rotary clubs and other community groups.

The couples sued in Vermont Superior Court. The burden of defending against the suit fell to the office of Attorney General William Sorrell, the son of Esther Sorrell, who had been Dean's political mentor when he first arrived in Vermont. William Sorrell had been elected the state's chief prosecutor just a few years earlier. The attorney general's office, which is independent of the governor's office and which is charged with defending state laws, argued that the state's constitution did not address the issue of marriage, so the constitution could not be applied in this case. Lawyers for the state also argued that the legislature had enacted the marriage statute to promote the link between procreation and child-rearing, to facilitate the transfer of property within families and to provide male and female role models for children.

Any changes to the marriage statutes, the attorney general

said, should be considered by the legislature, not the courts.

The lower-court judge sided with the state. She agreed that under the Vermont Constitution same-sex couples had no inherent right to marry. However, in her ruling, the judge rejected all but one of the state's reasons for limiting marriage to heterosexual couples. Protecting the link between procreation and child-rearing was the only argument she accepted.

The ruling rankled the couples. Baker's partner, Peter Harrigan, complained in a newspaper interview that, "We're being held to a standard that even heterosexuals are not held to. When you go to apply for a marriage license as a male-and-female couple, there's no piece of paper that you have to sign saying that you're planning to continue the [human] race." When Harrigan's grandmother remarried as an older woman, no one expected her to bear children.

Republican Rep. Thomas Little of Shelburne, a leading architect of the civil unions legislation, speaks to the House during debate on the bill in March 2000.
(Times-Argus *Photo by Jeb Wallace-Brodeur*)

The couples appealed to the Supreme Court, and the case drew increasingly widespread attention. Seventeen state and national groups wrote friend-of-the-court briefs either supporting or opposing the couples' case. Much was at stake for both sides. If the gay-rights movement had hoped to win the right to marry, Vermont seemed like a promising battleground.

One reason was that the five-member Vermont Supreme Court was widely seen as liberal. All of the justices had been appointed by Democratic governors. Dean had appointed two, including Chief Justice Jeffrey Amestoy, a former Republican attorney general who became so popular during his 12 years in office that Democrats stopped running candidates against him.

Conservative critics of the court said the justices acted like legislators and that they enjoyed nothing more than reading new rights into the state constitution.

In the Baker case, the court based its ruling on its reading of the Common Benefits Clause of the state's constitution, which was adopted in 1777. The clause declares "[t]hat government is, or ought to be, instituted for the common benefit, protection, and security of the people, nation, or community, and not for the particular emolument or advantage of any single person, family, or set of persons, who are a part only of that community."

To fulfill that requirement, Amestoy wrote, "We hold that the State is constitutionally required to extend to same-sex couples the common benefits and protections that flow from marriage under Vermont law." But the court said it was not the role of the judiciary to decide how to guarantee those benefits and protections. "Whether this ultimately takes the form of inclusion within the marriage laws themselves," Amestoy wrote, "or a parallel 'domestic partnership' system or some equivalent statutory alternative, rests with the Legislature. Whatever system is chosen, however, must conform with the constitutional imperative to afford all Vermonters the common benefit, protection, and security of the law."

The lone dissenting voice was that of Justice Denise Johnson, who felt the court had not gone far enough. Fifty years earlier, she noted, the California Supreme Court had struck down a law prohibiting interracial marriage; it didn't leave the job to the California legislature. Similarly, she argued, the Vermont Supreme Court should declare unconstitutional any future state law that would bar same-sex couples from marrying.

In concluding the ruling, Amestoy wrote that "[t]he extension of the Common Benefits Clause to acknowledge plaintiffs as Vermonters who seek nothing more, nor less, than legal protection and security for their avowed commitment to an intimate and lasting human relationship is simply, when all is said and done, a recognition of our common humanity."

IN THE SPOTLIGHT

Howard Dean looked out at a scrum of about 10 reporters and TV cameramen clustered around a large table at the Health Department. The governor began by saying he was pleased with the Vermont Supreme Court's ruling in the Baker case. He called it a "very elegant solution."

Now, he said, the legislature should respond by passing a domestic partnership bill — not a gay marriage bill — that would guarantee same-sex couples the same rights as married heterosexuals. If the legislature did that, Dean said, he would sign it.

"He wasn't on edge," recalls Adam Lisberg, then a reporter for the *Burlington Free Press,* the state's largest newspaper. "People have different modes of seriousness. At some press conferences, he was very playful with the press. At others, he was serious. He was serious at this one, but it wasn't like panic."

Peter Freyne, the political columnist for *Seven Days,* an alternative newspaper in Burlington, interpreted the governor's mood differently. "Howard Dean looked like a man whose political life just passed in front of his eyes," says Freyne, whose caustic and gossipy column is a must-read among Statehouse insiders. To Freyne, the mood at the news conference seemed depressing. "I felt like I was at a political wake," he says. "And [Dean] seemed to feel that way, too."

"His presidential aspirations had been public knowledge for some time, and he had steadfastly refused to give his position on gay marriage," Freyne says.

The columnist pressed Dean on the issue again that day.

"For three years you've ducked this," Freyne remembers saying. "Now it has been out of the courts for an hour, how do you feel?"

Dean's response did not sit well with Vermont's gay community, but it might have inadvertently helped him with others. "It makes me uncomfortable, the same as anybody else," Dean said.

The press picked up the remark and repeated it until it was

all that most people remembered about the news conference.

Lisberg, however, didn't use the comment in his front-page story the next day. "It looks bad in print, and it sounds bad now, but at the time I didn't think it seemed bad," he says. "It seemed like an unremarkable acknowledgment that this is uncharted territory for everybody, both legally and in the more sociological sense."

To Lisberg, Dean seemed to be saying, "'We are going to have to reconstruct our sense of what is family, what is morally right. It might be an uncomfortable adjustment, but we're going to have to do it.'

"Dean seemed to be saying there is a solution and this will work out. We're going to comply with the court. . . . Everyone ascribes it to his medical training. . . . But he is very good at laying down a statement of what is going to happen. He is very good at laying out options and summarizing what will happen very plainly, without a lot of emotion but with a lot of gravity."

Dean deflected journalists' questions about whether he would sign a gay marriage bill if lawmakers chose to go that route. "I think the Legislature will react with a domestic partnership bill and not a gay marriage bill," he said. "I'm comfortable with that — that's the best thing for Vermont."

Lisberg wasn't surprised to hear the governor suggesting how the process would end. "This is classic Dean; he is already thinking six months ahead," Lisberg says. "He wasn't going to worry about the legislative process. He knew what the result would be, and, of course, he was right."

Enduring the Backlash

As soon as the court issued its ruling in the Baker case, the phones began to ring in Gov. Dean's office. And it seemed they would never stop. Thousands of people outside the state wanted a say in the issue, and Dean worried that the pressure would distract legislators when they returned to the state capitol the first week of January.

"My greatest concern, frankly, about the legislative session is that outside groups will come in and try to manipulate the situation," he told reporters. "We've had about 150 calls in the first two days. A hundred twenty of them were out of state, and 22 were from in state.

"I think there are a lot of other people with agendas that have nothing to do with Vermont that, I hope, will not affect our legislature, because I do think there's a consensus among the folks that I've heard from."

> "Dean seemed to be saying there is a solution and this will work out. We're going to comply with the court."
>
> *Adam Lisberg,*
> *Former Burlington Free Press Reporter*

Those folks were presumably legislative leaders who agreed with Dean's assessment that some sort of domestic partnership bill was the best way to win lawmakers' final approval and also satisfy the court's requirements.

The majority of Vermonters, it seemed, didn't approve of gay marriage. A poll taken a month before the court decision found that 47 percent of Vermonters disapproved of same-sex marriage, while 40 percent approved. Gay-rights advocates, however, argued that polls were irrelevant in this kind of issue. Groups being discriminated against might have to wait forever for civil rights if it were up to the majority to grant them, they said.

The phones kept ringing, and Dean's office staff dutifully tallied the views of the callers. Soon, though, the office dispensed with the policy of answering each call with a letter. Only in-state calls would get such a response. That was because at the peak of the debate, the office, which normally would receive about 50 calls a day from constituents, was being swamped with at least 1,000.

"Everybody got pulled off their jobs to answer phones," remembers Sue Allen, Dean's press secretary at the time. The calls started to spike after a national conservative talk show host broadcast Dean's telephone number and told listeners to call his office. Gay-rights advocates countered by urging visitors to their Web sites to contact Dean.

The phone rang so often that when Dean was walking through the office, he sometimes picked up. "Governor's office," he would say and dutifully check off where the caller stood on the issue, never letting on who had answered the phone.

Sometimes the callers threatened the governor, either directly or obliquely. Most of the threats didn't bother Dean. "He almost seemed dismissive of them," says Allen. Then came the day a caller said he knew where Dean's children went to school. "That one concerned him deeply."

Most gay-rights opponents did not go that far. Bishop Kenneth Angell of the Catholic Diocese of Burlington issued statements and organized Statehouse vigils against gay marriage and domestic partnership. Fundamentalist Christian preachers railed against the ruling from their pulpits. Conservative commentators in Vermont complained that the justices (one took to calling them the "supreme legislators") had usurped the power of the legislature.

Gay-rights supporters also attacked Dean, mostly for his comments at the news conference after the ruling. "I heard it repeated within the gay community: 'I'm not comfortable. I'm not comfortable.' There was a mocking tone," remembers Bill Lippert, a Democratic House member from a town near Burlington, who at the time was the only openly gay member of the House.

Beth Robinson, one of the lawyers in the Baker case, says that before the court announced its decision, she considered Dean neutral on the case. "That's all we were looking for," Robinson says, but she was unhappy with the governor's response.

> Gay-rights supporters attacked Howard Dean, mostly for his comments at the news conference after the ruling.

"Once the decision came down, we had a more significant parting of ways with the governor, because the decision was kind of a half win, half loss," she says. "It was written in a way that how to react was open to interpretation. The governor was extremely quick on that. He was already saying let's do something less than marriage even before we had a chance to finish reading the decision. . . . We definitely were at odds with the governor. We very much wanted him to either stay out of the debate or to see the court's decision to its logical end [and support gay marriage], and he was very clear that he was not going to do either of those things."

LEGISLATORS GO TO WORK

If gay marriage was political lightning, Howard Dean wasn't the only one in danger of being struck.

Any bill responding to the court ruling would start in the House Judiciary Committee, where Tom Little, a Republican, was chairman. Little was mostly unknown to the public, but he was well respected in the Statehouse for his keen political instincts and his ability to build consensus. He would need all of his political skills to deal with this issue, and he knew it.

One night, shortly after the court's ruling, he was Christmas shopping on the bustling pedestrian mall in downtown Burlington when he bumped into Chief Justice Amestoy. Flashing a smile, the justice said, "Merry Christmas."

"We sort of shared a wink," Little recalls. "I knew what he went through, and he knew what I was about to go through."

Little also saw eye-to-eye with Dean. "We had this common vision of the type of legislation it would be," says Little, a lawyer and counsel for the state's Episcopal diocese. "I think we were both inclined to view things the same way: The only way to get the job accomplished and meet the court's requirements was to create a system that was not gay marriage." A majority of legislators would have opposed gay marriage.

Little didn't meet regularly with Dean. "If people in the building think you are just carrying the governor's water on something, you lose credibility," Little says. So most of his contacts with the governor came through chance encounters in the hallways of the Statehouse. When things got tough, however,

Little sometimes sought out Dean or his staff for moral support. "I didn't want to get too close to the governor," Little says, "and he didn't want to either in case [the legislation] blew up or ended up being a bill that was too close to gay marriage."

Besides, says Little, "I think he thought I knew how to run a committee."

Although Dean and Little saw a domestic partnership bill as the best political option, Little wanted to give his committee time to analyze the issue and consider the alternatives. Committee members immediately launched into an intensive study of the institution of marriage — reviewing its historical, social, legal and religious roots — and listened to scores of supporters and opponents of gay marriage. Speaking to the committee, Susan Murray, the lawyer for the Freedom to Marry Task Force, said the legislature should not pretend that domestic partnerships are equal to gay marriage. Such "partnerships" would be a second-class designation. What would happen, she asked, if married couples were suddenly told their marriages had been dissolved and replaced by domestic partnerships? "There would be an uproar. Those husbands and wives would feel they'd lost something," she said.

A lawyer for the Mormon Church urged lawmakers to amend the state constitution to ban same-sex marriages. "When it comes to marriage, we are dealing with the very hub of our social order," he told the committee. He also worried that same-sex marriage would open the door to people in less orthodox relationships seeking to marry. "What do you say tomorrow when three or more people say, 'We want to marry. We're in a committed relationship. We love each other'?"

A lawyer for Take It to the People, a Vermont group opposing gay marriage, urged lawmakers simply to ignore the court, since he said it had overreached its authority. The committee also heard from a professor of history and American studies from Yale University that our conception of marriage, "the particular arrangement of faithful monogamy on a Christian model between a man and a woman, authorized by the state," evolved in Western societies only in the early 1700s. Even in colonial

New England, she said, men and women often lived together without sanction from church or state.

The most dramatic testimony, however, wasn't from lawyers and academics sitting in the committee's cramped meeting room. It came during two nights of testimony from the general public before the House and Senate judiciary committees.

An hour before the first night's hearing, 500 people jammed the House chamber, an ornate, neoclassical room that normally seats 150 representatives at walnut desks and a few dozen visitors in rows of cushioned benches along a wall and in the balcony. By the time the testimony started, another 1,000 people crowded the building's hallways and hearing rooms. So many people were packed into the Statehouse that one senator worried the floor would collapse. More would have attended if not for a heavy snowstorm, which forced Bishop Angell to cancel a vigil planned for the Statehouse steps that night. Even in the snow, about 200 people gathered outside for a prayer rally.

Inside, people wishing to speak put their names in a box for the committee to draw at random. Each witness had two minutes to testify. Little warned the crowd at the start that "the rules of the assembly require that we all behave ourselves." And for the most part, they did. People wearing stickers reading "Don't Mock Marriage" sat quietly beside others with stickers saying "I Support Freedom to Marry."

During her two minutes, one opponent of both gay marriage and domestic partnerships, said: "God made Adam and Eve, not Adam and Steve." Another opponent asked legislators, "Is this really what we want Vermont to be famous for?"

A former minister, during his testimony, said, "I say let the religious debate be just that — a healthy religious debate . . . within congregations, within families. Changing the law in Vermont won't stop that debate, but it will correct the current situation of institutional discrimination."

Another supporter of gay marriage said: "Here's a litmus test to tell you when you've created an equal system. When everyone in this room is comfortable trading in their marriage license for whatever the new system is, then you've got it."

During January, while the House Judiciary Committee was considering the issue, Dean held several strategy meetings with a half-dozen Democratic leaders in his ceremonial corner office at the Statehouse, a formal room with a long rectangular table and red velvet chairs.

The conversations were frank and brief. No one wasted time discussing the dangers of supporting gay marriage or anything like it. "People knew there were political risks," says then-House Speaker Michael Obuchowski, a burly legislator with a thick moustache. "We understood that it might explode." Obie, as he was known around the state, had already been in the Legislature for 27 years but had never seen a more contentious issue.

As the legislative session progressed, he and his fellow Democrats continued to worry about how to proceed. The House Judiciary Committee already had considered gay marriage politically unfeasible, so now lawmakers were debating whether to back a domestic partnership bill, or simply delay the whole question for further study. That would get everyone past the fall's elections. But they felt they had to make some kind of decision. The

Lois Farnham and Holly Puterbaugh speak with an international group of reporters after receiving their civil union license in South Burlington the day the law went into effect. Farnham and Puterbaugh were one of three plaintiff couples involved in the State Supreme Court decision that led to the law.
(Times-Argus *Photo by Jeb Wallace-Brodeur*)

Supreme Court had issued a ruling, but the justices also had reserved their right to impose gay marriage, or some other remedy, if the legislature failed to find a solution.

"One side of the fulcrum was what was politically expedient, and on the other side was the right thing to do,"

Obuchowski says. He recalls Dean's advice. "'This is something we need to do, and we need to do it as fast as we can.' He never said to us, 'Don't do it, it's political suicide, it's the wrong thing, or I'm uncomfortable, or go slow, do a study.'"

Neither the speaker nor the other House leaders ordinarily looked to Dean for advice. They were more used to fighting with him over his tight budgets and other issues. But in this case, they wanted his guidance. "All of us were looking to Howard Dean for leadership, and especially for political judgment," Obuchowski says. "We couldn't see all the field, but he could. Maybe he had more information coming to him or maybe he was able to process the information better than us."

Dean and Little proved correct in their political calculations. No more than 35 representatives out of 150 would have supported gay marriage, Little says. On the other extreme, a bill to amend the constitution to ban gay marriage drew only 12 co-sponsors.

After weeks of grueling testimony, Little's committee voted formally to draft a domestic partnership bill. The committee's bill took the state's marriage law and used it as the basis of a new system that the committee dubbed "civil unions." The bill would grant each partner in a civil union the rights associated with civil marriage, such as those involving hospital visits, medical decisions, health insurance coverage, inheritance and funeral arrangements. The law, of course, would not infringe on how churches defined marriage. Neither the federal government nor other states would be bound to recognize civil unions.

The House Judiciary Committee then sent a version of the civil unions bill to the full House, where it passed by seven votes. Many representatives in voicing support for the measure during floor debate said voting for civil unions would cost them their legislative seats in the next election. "We thought we had the votes," Obuchowski says, "but when people are voting their conscience, you never know."

By the time the bill reached the Senate, opposition was growing more angry.

Vince Illuzzi, a Republican senator known for his constituent service, remembers the tension. One day, Illuzzi found himself in a screaming match on the telephone with a constituent. The argument ended with Illuzzi slamming down the receiver. Another senator who overheard the exchange exclaimed, "Jesus Christ! Who was that?"

"That was one of my longtime supporters," Illuzzi answered dejectedly.

Members of the Senate Judiciary Committee took to the road with their public hearings, first facing fierce opposition to the bill in socially conservative St. Albans in the far northwestern corner of the state, near the Canadian border. "The opponents of civil unions were pretty vicious that night," says Dick Sears, the committee's chairman, who had promised that his panel would not simply rubber stamp the House bill. There was no pleasing the crowd. "That tipped the scales on the committee," says Sears. "We desperately sought some way to compromise, but there was no way [civil unions opponents] were going to compromise on this. No way."

So committee members stopped looking for ways to appease gay-rights opponents, Sears says.

A second hearing was held in Sears' hometown of Bennington, at the opposite end of Vermont, near the border with Massachusetts and New York. Take It to the People tried to demonstrate all the discontent in Sears' back yard, he says, and members put fliers in the local newspaper urging opponents to attend. "It kind of backfired on them," he says. "I'd say proponents outnumbered opponents three-to-one at that one. What it proved was that the state really was split."

The committee took nearly a month to vote out a slightly modified version of the House bill to the full Senate. Among other changes, the Senate tried to allay fears that civil unions were gay marriages in disguise by writing into the bill, in three places, declarations that marriage would remain a partnership between a man and a woman.

Sears felt tremendous pressure, but says Dean's encouragement and belief that civil unions were a civil rights issue helped him do his job. "I felt, as someone who was really in the hot seat for a couple of months there, that I had support in the corner office [from Dean]," Sears says.

The Senate approved the bill by a vote of 19–11. After the House approved the Senate's modifications, only Dean's signature was needed.

SIGNING IN PRIVATE

Howard Dean rested his head on his hands as he sat at a table. All his aides had filed out of the room except his press secretary, Susan Allen, who always briefed him before news conferences. But Dean didn't want to talk this time, and he had declined Allen's offer to write a statement. He wanted to speak from the heart, not from a piece of paper. For 10 minutes, Allen sat silently as Dean collected his thoughts. From his ceremonial office two doors away came the hum of conversation as legislators and reporters awaited Dean. They were there, they assumed, to watch the governor sign the civil unions bill into law. Now Dean was going to have to go in there and explain why he had already signed the bill a half hour earlier.

The signing had been simple and private. Before a group of about a dozen aides and a handful of cabinet members, Dean had talked about the significance of the legislation and explained why he was shunning a public ceremony. And then he had signed it.

Shortly afterward, he summoned the chairmen of the legislature's judiciary committees, Dick Sears and Tom Little, and their two vice chairmen, and repeated what he had said to his staff moments before. Now Dean was about to deliver the same message for the third time in half an hour. This time it would be in a more formal way and under bright television lights.

Reporters chatted as they awaited Dean's arrival. "The tip ahead of time was the governor was going to sign the bill," recalls Peter Freyne, the political columnist. "This was all people were talking about during that legislative session. This wasn't just the center of the universe, it was the universe. Mad dogs and Englishmen were descending on that building that day, and people were saying, 'He is going to sign the bill.'"

Finally, Dean stood from his chair, cut past a receptionist's desk and stepped into his ceremonial office. He walked to the podium and began to speak.

"At about 1:30 this afternoon, with my staff, I signed the civil unions bill," he began. The press was stunned. Reporters and photographers had expected to witness and record a historic moment, but Dean had changed the script. The journalists began grumbling. They felt cheated. Why had the governor decided to sign this, of all bills, behind closed doors?

Dean, during his eight-minute speech, focused mostly on a different question — why he considered the bill important. His words, at first awkward, left no doubt where he stood.

"I chose to sign this bill because I fundamentally believe it's the right thing to do . . ." he said. "I believe that because until every human being is treated with dignity, because they are a human being, and not because they belong in some category, then every American and every Vermonter is poorer. . . . This bill enriches not just the very small percentage of gay and lesbian Vermonters who take advantage of this partnership and get the rights that the court has determined that they are due. I believe this bill enriches all of us, as we look with new eyes at a group of people who have been outcasts for many, many generations."

He spoke of the rending process the state had been through. "This is a bill that is about the deepest, most personal feelings that human beings have. I personally have friends, supporters, that are furious with me over the fact that I have supported this bill. And I know that I have disappointed them, and that's a very painful feeling. I, like many of the people in this building, have not had a great deal of sleep for the past five months."

Then, he tried to explain why the signing had been private. "In politics, bill signings are triumphant. They represent the overcoming of one side over the other; they're a cause for celebration. There is much to celebrate about this bill. Those celebrations, as the subject matter of this bill, will be private. They will be celebrated by couples and their families, by people making commitments to each other."

In closing, Dean reached out to the bill's opponents. "There is no shame in having opposed this bill for most of the people who opposed it," he said. "We will now use the time to reconcile each other's viewpoints. But we will go forth forever more realizing that equality is not simply a matter of a concept that's written in history books; equality of opportunity, equality of treatment, equal access to the law, equal respect for the law, has been this year a living process in this state."

> "I chose to sign this bill because I fundamentally believe it's the right thing to do."
>
> *Howard Dean,*
> *April 26, 2000*

Despite Dean's talk of historic moments, the press reacted with anger and frustration.

"He gave an amazing, impassioned speech. There were a lot of people in there who were crying," says Christopher Graff, correspondent for the Associated Press in Montpelier. "Even though the journalists were moved by what he said, they were so upset that they had been cut out of the signing, and they felt he'd taken the cheap way out."

Dean said he wanted to "extend a hand" to the law's opponents and to avoid further alienating them. "We are never going to succeed in bringing people together if we brand all people who opposed this bill as bigots," he said. "It's just never going to work. This bill only works if we bring the opponents back to accept this. No law can change people's hearts."

A reporter suggested the private signing sent the message that gays and lesbians are second-class citizens. The remark struck a nerve. "I can't imagine any governor in this country who would take the position that I've taken on this bill," he retorted. "In fact, there hasn't been one. But I also think it's important to acknowledge there are two very strongly divided sides in this debate, and I think sometimes signing ceremonies take on the trappings of triumphalism. That was not appropriate in this case."

Reporters suggested that Dean feared his opponents would have used a photo of the signing to attack him in the coming election. Dean rolled his eyes and said he wasn't worried about that.

The signing behind closed doors angered others as well. Gay-rights advocates and opponents both said they thought the governor should have stood up more publicly for what he believed.

> "If he was a homophobe, he probably could have stuffed [the legislation]. He let the process work. He was smart enough to keep his hands off that process and let it work."
>
> *Stephen Kimbell,*
> *Montpelier Lobbyist*

"I voted against it, but I still respect people who voted for it. For or against it, be how you are, but just stay on your principles," says Republican Connie Houston, then the House minority whip. "Governor Dean was non-existent during this whole debate because it was political suicide in Vermont and he knew that."

The civil unions bill had no greater foe than George Schiavone, a mellow-voiced, white-haired Republican who represented a district near Burlington. Schiavone helped organize the Traditional Marriage Caucus, which claimed nearly half the House members at one point. Though the caucus was staunchly opposed to gay marriage, when civil unions were offered as a compromise, some members broke ranks and helped pass the bill.

"Overall, I'd say [Dean] was not involved to any degree at all in that whole subject. He watched as the legislature sent the thing back and forth," Schiavone says. "When it moved along, people tried to figure out what he was going to do. He didn't twist any arms on that like he did on some other things. Governor Dean is one of the best politicians I've ever seen. I never saw a person who politically knew better how to do things. But I'm sure that day he wondered whether that was the end of him."

Others witnessed Dean at the Statehouse and came to the opposite conclusion. Stephen Kimbell watched the debate daily as a lobbyist for the Freedom to Marry Task Force. "The governor didn't have someone assigned to this issue in terms of affecting what was getting written," says Kimbell. "He gets lots of notoriety for not being more involved, but that's not what governors do. What governors do is try to drive their agenda through the legislature, which is mostly the budget. But this wasn't his issue. He didn't ask for this. It got dropped in his lap."

Kimbell describes Dean's role as pivotal. "If he was a homophobe, he probably could have stuffed [the legislation]," he says. "He let the process work. He was smart enough to keep his hands off that process and let it work."

Some saw Dean's private signing as the act of a politician desperate to hang on to his job. But Freyne saw it as a politician angling for a new one.

"When he comes out and says, I already signed the bill, I said quietly to myself, you've got to be kidding me," Freyne says. "Then I realized, he's [considering] running for president. If you make the logical connection, you realize that if you're Howard Dean, you don't want to have anyone, particularly the Republicans, have a picture of you signing a bill legalizing gay marriage — you can forget the semantics, that's what he did."

In the five months between the Baker decision and the signing of the civil unions bill, Freyne noticed a transformation in Dean. "He looked like death warmed over at the press conference after the ruling," Freyne says. "Now he seemed to be saying, 'I ain't dead yet.'"

MORE BACKLASH

The bill signing on April 26 unleashed a new flood of calls and letters to the governor's office.

"I was really sorry to read where you have allowed the passage of a bill recognizing queers to marry," wrote one Kentucky resident, who vowed never to vacation in Vermont again. "I have been a Democrat all my life, but now that the Democrats are turning into queers, I am switching to the Republican Party. I hope you and all your queer buddies rot in hell."

Another came addressed to "Governor Dean, Homosexual Lover." Inside, it said, "Dean Is A Faggot Lover. All Homosexuals, Go to Vermont, Dean Loves You. All Normal People, Stay Away From Vermont. A State Full Of Perverts — Run By Perverts. Boycott Fag Run Vermont."

Others took a more civil tone in opposing civil unions.

"I will take this opportunity to express my deep concern that the passage of this type of bill only undermines the ethics and values that our country was built on and more importantly, the moral standard of the institution of marriage," wrote a woman from Florida.

But Dean also received many praising him for signing the bill into law.

"In the 45 years since I moved to Vermont I have always been proud to be a Vermonter, but I am especially proud now that you have signed the Civil Union bill into law," wrote one man. "Thank you for having the courage to do what is right for all people in this state. . . . I speak as a retired superintendent of schools who has been happily married to my same wife for 47 years. In no way do I feel threatened by this new law."

REACTION FROM GAYS

Beth Robinson, the lawyer who argued the Baker case for the three couples, received both flowers in celebration and cards of condolence on the day the decision was announced. Just as the state's gay community was divided on how to respond to the ruling, Robinson felt conflicted about Dean's actions.

"I give Governor Dean solidly mixed marks," she says. "I am critical of Governor Dean for embracing a position of less than equality and claiming he is the civil rights guy for gay folks. But I am proud of Governor Dean for the way he didn't back down and tried to educate people."

Robinson felt undercut when Dean, immediately after the court ruling, jumped at the solution that would become civil unions, rather than consider the option of gay marriage. In the end, the Freedom to Marry Task Force had to settle for less than the freedom to marry.

"Once it was clear that marriage was off the table and the choice was whether to get behind civil unions or not, we, after extensive debate, decided to get behind the bill," she says. "We could no longer focus our energies on opposing Governor Dean. At that point, our interests and views merged for the balance of the legislative session."

Dean, she says, was trying to anger the fewest people while still addressing the court's mandate. "He found what he thought was going to be a middle path and he pushed that hard. . . . He was the strongest advocate for that path, and at the time no one else was pushing. The anti-gay community was opposed to an thing that recognizes same-sex couples and affords them equal rights." Dean was wrong, Robinson says, to assume that gay-rights opponents would accept civil unions as a compromise. "They didn't have any constituency that said, give them half a loaf."

Rep. Bill Lippert, the gay legislator, is more forgiving. Without Howard Dean, he says, civil unions would never have become law. Advocates of gay marriage fixated on Dean's comment that same-sex marriage made him "uncomfortable" and were angry. But Lippert prefers to focus on the rest of what the governor said that day. "He also said that 'I support legislation that codifies what the Supreme Court ruled were the constitutional rights of lesbian and gay couples and I will sign that bill,'" Lippert says. "The governor made it clear there wasn't going to be a veto at the end of the road. I don't think House and Senate leaders and members would have put themselves through what they went through if he hadn't said what he did."

Lippert has had to defend Dean from attacks by members of the gay community over the "uncomfortable" comment and the closed-door signing of the bill.

"I say to them, this governor, more than any governor in the history of this country, put his career on the line for the most important bill ever for the lesbian and gay community, and I don't think he deserves to have that questioned," he says.

Immediately after Dean announced he had signed the bill, reporters approached Lippert as he left the ceremonial office. "They descended on me and they were clearly looking at me for a statement from me that I was disappointed," he recalls. "That was clearly going to be the headline. I was frustrated that this monumental achievement was going to be overlooked over the question of how he signed it."

Then Lippert made a decision. "I remember walking away from the governor's office six or ten paces and then deciding I was going to go back to the governor and give a different tone to the day. I went into his office, found the governor and shook his hand."

This was an accomplishment to celebrate, Lippert says, and that public handshake "was my attempt to put that on the front page."

Mark Bushnell

Gov. Howard Dean and U.S. Sen. Patrick
Leahy pass a "Take Back Vermont" sign
while touring renovated homes
in Rutland. The sign's message
was the battle cry of the
anti–civil unions movement.
(Rutland Herald *Photo by Vyto Starinskas*)

CHAPTER 8

Skillful, Feisty in His Campaigns

Three months after he signed the civil unions bill into law Howard Dean had to walk the plank. On a late-July evening in 2000, Art Ristau, a former state and city official, had invited the mayor of Barre and four of the mayor's predecessors, along with people from his neighborhood, to meet the governor at a backyard gathering. Dean was in his fifth and final race for governor, and the campaign was a tough one.

Dean knew that Barre, though a Democratic stronghold, would not provide the most hospitable audience for a governor who, by signing the civil unions bill into law, had just struck the final blow in what many saw as an egregious assault on marriage.

A city of 9,300, Barre is a working-class town of largely Italian and French-Canadian Catholics whose ancestors had come to cut the prized granite from the steep hills outside of town. Barre is just eight miles from Montpelier, and the two communities are sometimes referred to as the Twin Cities. But if they are twins, they are not identical. Montpelier is a government and professional town, its business district sprinkled with trendy restaurants and boutiques. With 8,000 residents, the nation's smallest state capital carries the dubious distinction of having the second highest number of lawyers per capita of any U.S. city, behind Washington, D.C. Barre, by contrast, is proud of its blue-collar, stonecutters' heritage. A reporter once summed up the difference between the two cities by saying that Montpelier is a place where people shower in the morning and Barre is a place where they shower in the evening. Barre's pride can be seen in the Hope Cemetery, just north of downtown, where people of modest means are buried beneath ornate memorials carved by their survivors. Angels, crucifixes, saints and other symbols of Roman Catholic devotion are beautifully carved in gray granite.

In this city, social conservatism born in religious devotion blends with a labor liberalism left over from the early 20th century, when Barre was a hotbed of New England radicalism. The socialist Eugene Debs, anarchist Emma Goldman and the labor activist Mary Harris "Mother" Jones were among the speakers who addressed large crowds at the Barre Opera House. Many immigrants' sons and daughters had worked their way up into the middle class, but they still strongly identified with the Democratic Party's look-out-for-the-little-guy ethos.

Culturally, however, many of these Democrats are conservative, a reality that didn't escape Dean.

The night Dean went to Barre, more than two dozen citizens had crowded onto Ristau's 16-by-12-foot stone patio, and Ristau decided he needed some elevation to deliver his welcoming remarks. So he stepped up onto the diving board of his swimming pool in order to be seen by everyone in the group. When Ristau finished and stepped back down onto the patio, Dean strode out onto the diving board and took his place. "He was wearing a shirt and tie," is the first thing Ristau recalls, "a white shirt about two sizes too small in the neck and a red tie. He had taken his jacket off."

Dean thanked his host for the introduction. He talked a bit about the history of the modern Democratic Party in Vermont, beginning in the 1960s, when the election of Gov. Phil Hoff, who was also a guest that evening, broke a century-long string of Republican rule in the state. He talked about his own accomplishments as governor. Then he shifted to the topic on everyone's minds.

Dean reminded the group of the constitutional duty of the governor and legislature to respond to rulings of the courts. He and lawmakers had been ordered to revamp Vermont's public school finance system after the state Supreme Court ruled in 1997 that children in communities with little taxable property were not getting an education equal to those from richer communities. Similarly, Dean and lawmakers were required to respond to the court's ruling that gay and lesbian couples have the same legal rights and responsibilities as married couples. "He talked about the rule of law and how it is emblematic of what Vermont stands for and for what's significant in our political life," Ristau says. Dean then invited questions. Most were polite; many were pointed.

Dean easily won Ristau's neighbor, Collette Carbonneau, back into his camp. "I do like Governor Dean a lot," the 73-year-old granite craftsman's widow confides three years after the event. "I think he's done a good job. He's very personable. He works hard at that."

But Dean was not so successful with another neighbor, who asked that she not be identified. "I was brought up in my day with very religious ways," adds this neighbor, 64, also a granite worker's widow. "My parents set very high morals. We always believed that a marriage was between a man and a woman. . . ."

She is not a Dean supporter today — probably because of civil unions. "If he would have opposed this, I might feel differently," she says. "He's done some good things, like children's health programs. He balanced the budget. . . . Hey, that's great. I wish the federal government would do that." And she gives Dean credit for appearing that night in Barre and defending his civil unions decision in a forthright manner. "He's very courageous," she says.

Dean's trip to Barre was one of dozens he made around Vermont that summer and fall in which he had asked his hosts to gather people who were unhappy with him. The aim was to let citizens vent and to give them a sense someone in power was listening to them. The sessions were held in backyards and living rooms and barns. Some participants likened the events to group therapy. The media were not invited, so Dean got no publicity and most voters didn't even know they were being held. The truth be told, they very likely saved Howard Dean's political skin. He went on to win the election of 2000 by the barest of margins. He just managed to top the 50 percent threshold that was needed to keep the election out of what in January 2001 — because of fallout from the civil unions bill — would be a Republican-dominated legislature.

Under the Vermont Constitution, if no candidate for governor gets at least 50 percent of the vote, the election is decided by a joint assembly of the House and Senate. This was a huge worry for Dean in 2000, as he faced challenges from both the right and the left. To his right was Republican Ruth Dwyer, a conservative firebrand who had represented the Connecticut River Valley town of Thetford in the Vermont House, and who had already run once against Dean — in 1998. To his left was Anthony Pollina of the Progressive Party, an unusually strong third party that had criticized Dean and the Democrats for failing to do enough to protect Vermont's poor.

> Political campaigns in Vermont are usually exercises in polite discourse. For the most part, Vermonters take pride in their democratic traditions and their inclination to disagree respectfully.

Pollina, a New Jersey native who had been active in Vermont politics for two decades, decided to run in the late fall of 1999, before the Vermont Supreme Court handed down its Baker decision. It had looked as though Dean was headed toward another easy victory, and Pollina, a longtime activist and organizer on agriculture, peace and other issues, wanted the Progressives to at least have a voice in the election. Pollina had come to Vermont in the 1970s for college. He had been active in politics since the early 1980s, running unsuccessfully against U.S. Rep. Jim Jeffords in 1984.

Pollina in 2000 had shoulder-length hair that suggested a 1960s radical, but he had support across the political spectrum. He had a clear and deliberate style of speaking that made voters pay attention.

Pollina says he decided to run against Dean "because there were a lot of issues that were not being addressed . . . particularly the basic economic issues. . . . There's the fact that Vermont is a low-wage state [and] the fact that we have the most expensive state colleges in the country. We were and are continuing to lose our agriculture. . . . I was the only one who spoke consistently about the number of Vermonters who aren't receiving a livable wage."

As he declared his candidacy for governor at a Progressive state convention in November 1999, it did not occur to Pollina that he might become a spoiler and help to elect a conservative Republican as governor. "When you enter a political campaign, you enter it to win and speak your mind," he says.

Pollina, interviewed in the late summer of 2003, says he saw irony in Dean's apparent move to the left as he made the transition from governor to presidential candidate. Dean has been rallying with striking telephone workers and talking about narrowing the growing gap between rich and poor, and Pollina says he, and not Dean, was the one articulating these sorts of issues in 2000. "Dean is running a very smart campaign," Pollina says. "One thing that's smart is he's appealing to those same basic issues."

POLITICS, VERMONT STYLE

Political campaigns in Vermont are usually exercises in polite discourse. For the most part, Vermonters take pride in their democratic traditions and their inclination to disagree respectfully. There's a state holiday where that tradition is celebrated: It's called Town Meeting Day, and it's held on the first Tuesday in March. On that day, ordinary citizens go down to the town hall or to the school auditorium and play legislator for a day, deciding whether the firehouse needs a new roof, the roads need paving or whether the town should contribute to the regional battered women's shelter. State legislative districts are tiny by national standards: House members represent about 3,800 people, senators about 21,000. By contrast, each of California's 80 Assembly members represents about 431,000. Rank-and-file Vermont lawmakers have no individual staffs, so the best way to reach them is to call them at home or corner them at the town recycling center on Saturday morning. Statehouse politics in Vermont usually is a game of softball in which Democratic House speakers appoint at least a few Republican committee chairs and governors retain high officials who served predecessors from the opposing party.

There's also a strain of quirky surrealism and street theater to Vermont politics. Vermonters are apt to balk at big money, lampoon opportunists and laugh at themselves.

The best Vermont example of real politics mimicking absurdist art occurred in 1998, in the Republican primary for U.S. Senate. It featured Fred Tuttle, a retired dairy farmer from the town of Tunbridge, and Jack McMullen, a wealthy Massachusetts resident who had a summer home in Vermont, but who had just moved to the state permanently. McMullen figured he could win the GOP primary and then have a go at Democratic incumbent Patrick Leahy.

Tuttle was known across the state because he had just played himself in a home-grown film spoof about a Vermont farmer who — as a candidate on the "Regressive Party" ticket — won a seat in Congress by running an honest campaign against a political sleaze. The movie, *Man With A Plan,* became a cult classic.

When McMullen surfaced as a candidate, the film's mischievous creator, John O'Brien, urged Tuttle to run in the primary. Tuttle defeated McMullen in what was probably the state's most entertaining election, and then he promptly endorsed Leahy.

The state has had other colorful characters, including a few national figures. George Aiken is remembered not only for his famous remark about how to save face and exit Vietnam, but also for having spent only $17.09 on his 1968 re-election campaign, which, of course, he won. Sen. James Jeffords, whose departure from the Republican Party in 2001 stunned the Bush administration and gave Democrats control of the Senate, made a name for himself with his living arrangements in Washington as a young House member in the 1970s. To save money, he camped out in his office for a time and lived in a travel trailer. And then there's Bernie Sanders, Vermont's only congressman. As a socialist with a small "s," he won his first congressional election with the support of gun-owner groups.

> No opponent in Howard Dean's three previous campaigns for governor, in 1992, 1994 and 1996, had ever posed a serious threat, and none ended up with as much as 30 percent of the vote.

But while Vermont's political fabric has a thread of comedy and innocent iconoclasm, real frustration and anger crop up now and then. A cultural divide exists that sometimes expresses itself in disputes between deer hunter and animal lover; logger and environmentalist; property-rights defender and "smart-growth" advocate. It occasionally flares between Vermont natives, with their rural traditions, and the non-native "flatlanders," who came to Vermont looking to make a better world — at least in one small part of it.

The natives won in 1986 when the House rejected a bill endorsed by animal-rights groups that would have banned the use of leg-hold traps for fur-bearing animals. The newcomers won two years later when the legislature passed a law calling for new regional land-use plans. The culture war subsided a bit for the next few years as the state struggled with budget deficits and two gubernatorial transitions. But in 1997 it re-emerged with a vengeance as lawmakers passed new regulations putting restrictions on logging clearcuts of more than 40 acres. Then came the state's participation in the Champion lands project in the Northeast Kingdom. The land could be hunted and fished, hiked and canoed, but restrictions were placed on logging and development. Rural anger simmered in the 1997 legislative session; it boiled in the gubernatorial election of 1998, and it boiled over in 2000.

RUTH DWYER'S EMERGENCE

It was during the 1997 legislative debate on the clearcutting law that Rep. Ruth Dwyer gained her first statewide headlines. Ohio-born, well spoken, attractive, stylish in hair and dress, Dwyer at first seemed an unlikely champion of flannel-shirted loggers and hardscrabble farmers. But she got their attention when, during House debate on the logging bill, she likened government encroachments on rural traditions to the early stages of the Nazi Holocaust. She said Europe's Jews adopted a stance that said, "'If we go along, if we don't resist, if we just let them do this little thing we don't like, then they'll leave us alone.' Well, we all know that didn't happen. It didn't work for them. It's not going to work for our landowners. I know that. History repeats itself."

Liberals thought Dwyer was being insensitive at best, an anti-Semite at worst, to equate the Holocaust in any way to the regulation of logging in Vermont. But Dwyer developed a following, and in April 1998, at the urging of some of her fellow conservatives in the House, she declared her first candidacy for governor. She told a reporter that she had decided to jump into the race on the spur of the moment, in part to rally her fellow Republicans, who were dispirited after losing several legislative skirmishes to the majority Democrats. Dwyer seemed to speak for both her GOP House colleagues and her rural constituency when she said, "I just felt it was worth going out and doing something for the people who've been doing the work and not getting any credit for it."

The "forgotten Vermonter," as Dwyer came to call the people she sought to represent, had emerged with a bang four months before Dwyer's announcement. It came in the form of a protest — legal to be sure — but one that tested Vermont's self-image of political comity.

Just hours after the feisty liberal state senator Cheryl Rivers of Stockbridge had sold a 10-year-old Dodge Colt wagon for $200, the old car turned up on tree-lined State Street in front of the Statehouse. A big sign on it read "Cheryl's Car," and a group of loggers and property-rights activists, unhappy with her liberal politics, were taking turns battering it with sledgehammers. It cost $5 a whack, with the proceeds going toward a new property-rights group called POST — Property Owners Standing Together.

The protest made good pictures for television news, and the incident shocked many Vermonters, eventually becoming a subject for debate in the 1998 campaign.

Dwyer had said in January in a speech to the Vermont Forest Products Association that, "The time has come to make yourselves a little dangerous." And the destruction of a

Republican gubernatorial candidate Ruth Dwyer makes a point during a debate with Gov. Howard Dean.
(Times-Argus *Photo by Jeb Wallace-Brodeur*)

car that just hours before had belonged to one of the property-rights activists' most-hated lawmakers was designed to send a message containing more than a hint of menace.

"It was a bit intimidating," Rivers says. "The woman who bought it said it was for her teenage son. "It burned a little oil," Rivers notes, and her husband, Richard, promised to help the young man keep it running. When the Riverses saw the car being sledge-hammered on the news that night, Richard Rivers' comment was: "There goes the guarantee all to hell."

No opponent in Dean's three previous campaigns for governor, in 1992, 1994 and 1996, had ever posed a serious threat, and none ended up with as much as 30 percent of the vote. Dean knew that in 1998 he would face serious opposition for the first time. He had more than the loggers and other defenders of property rights to worry about. Thanks to the Supreme Court ruling on school funding, there was also Act 60, the new school finance law that sought to equalize school property taxes around the state. That new law meant that property taxes would be raised sharply in towns where historically they had been very low.

Dean was under pressure, and he responded to it in the blunt, and at times ungraceful, fashion for which he has become known. Late in the campaign, Dwyer expressed annoyance that the governor seemed to be making more visits than usual around the state to hand out state grant checks to libraries and other local institutions. Dean responded: "I don't run around the state with a big bag of money during election time. I do that all the time." Notwithstanding his problem with logic, Dean's "I do that all the time" comment actually scored points with voters who admired his frankness.

And on a larger level, Dean worked to preserve more important forms of grace and civility in Vermont political life against what he and some others perceived as a growing threat. Vermont's political climate, even in 1998, was tame in comparison with what's come to be expected in many other states. Dean wanted to keep it that way. If no one spoke out against

Moments after receiving the concession call from Ruth Dwyer, Gov. Howard Dean shares a laugh with 85-year-old Helen Simino, a longtime supporter.
(Times-Argus *Photo by Jeb Wallace-Brodeur)*

behavior like sledge-hammering a car in front of the State-house, such conduct could worsen, he argued. He took Dwyer to task for urging her supporters to "make yourselves a little dangerous." That language "is not appropriate for government officials of any kind," he told a reporter. "You get the kind of thing that went on in Buffalo and you get the kind of thing that went on in Wyoming," referring to the murders of a Buffalo-area doctor who performed abortions and a gay student who was beaten by bigots in Laramie. "Government officials cannot use incendiary language, no matter how strongly they feel about an issue," Dean said.

Dean talked up "the civility issue" in the waning days of the campaign and it worked. He ended up winning the 1998 election with 56 percent of the vote.

THE 2000 CAMPAIGN

Ruth Dwyer began the rematch campaign in 2000 with a demand to be heard. "The big, overarching [issue] that I hear over and over again from people . . . is nobody's listening anymore, and we'd like our government to listen to us," Dwyer declared as she kicked off her campaign in the backyard of a suburban Burlington gas station owned by a party activist. "It's about time we put some people back up there that know how to listen."

Meanwhile, with civil unions an issue, rural anger had begun to manifest itself in a new way. Richard Lambert, a farmer from the town of Washington, about 25 miles southeast of Montpelier, came up with a three-word slogan to sum up the outrage he and many like-minded Vermonters felt. Logging restrictions, land-use planning and other liberal social inventions were one thing, but having their state offer an official public approval for homosexual relationships was going too far. Together with friends, Lambert ordered 5,000 copies of a sign, four feet long and two feet tall, with 5½-inch black block letters on a white background. It said simply, "Take Back Vermont."

The Take Back Vermont signs appeared on barn walls, porch railings and fence posts across rural Vermont. Some of the tourists who came that fall to see Vermont's spectacular foliage thought the signs were urging them to take home Vermont maple syrup or cheddar cheese. But the intent of the sign-writers was much more serious. Soon, supporters of the civil unions bill responded by having smaller, green signs and bumper stickers printed saying "Take Vermont Forward" or "Keep Vermont Civil." But perhaps because of their size, their stark, black-on-white coloring, their ubiquity in some communities and the anger they reflected, Lambert's signs seemed to pack a more powerful punch.

Sensing Dean's vulnerability over the civil unions issue and seeing an opportunity to end the political career of a Democrat who wanted to be president, the Republican National Committee promised to pump big money into Dwyer's campaign. Vermont historically had been a cheap place to run for office. Television advertising was seen as less effective than elsewhere, because Vermont's mountains interfered with broadcast reception and cable wasn't available in most rural areas. Until recent years a quarter-million dollars could buy a respectable, even winning, campaign for governor. But when the RNC promised an open checkbook for Dwyer, the Democratic National Committee responded in kind for Dean. Dean and Dwyer ended up raising nearly $1 million each, and both got more than half their money from their national parties.

ANGER IN ST. ALBANS

Dean knew he faced a bumpy road, but he didn't know how rough it would be until he traveled to St. Albans for the annual Maple Festival. It was held in June, less than two months after he had signed the civil unions bill.

Frank Cioffi, a St. Albans native who had served as Dean's economic development commissioner, was to be the governor's host for his visit to the fading railroad city and county seat in Vermont's northwest corner. The governor normally traveled with a single state trooper who acted as driver and bodyguard. But six accompanied him to St. Albans, Cioffi recalls. "I talked with a couple of the state troopers. They were really nervous. There had been a number of threats," he says. The day would begin with a fund-raising walk for a much-loved local high school teacher who was suffering from brain cancer. As they gathered in a parking lot north of downtown to begin the walk,

Cioffi offered Dean a special T-shirt that had been printed in the teacher's honor. The governor said it would be difficult for him to put on. "The state police want me to wear this damn vest," he told Cioffi. The vest was bulletproof. The fact that Vermont's governor traveled the state that summer and fall wearing a bulletproof vest was not known publicly until well after the 2000 election.

> "People would not make eye contact with him, and these were people who had supported him strongly in the past."
>
> *Frank Cioffi,*
> *Former Economic Development*
> *Commissioner*

Dean had always done well in St. Albans and the rest of Franklin County, a conservative Democratic bastion with Lake Champlain to the west and the province of Quebec to the north. In this center of Vermont's dairy farming industry, Dean had won around 70 percent of the vote in his previous four elections. The Maple Festival usually provided a friendly environment for the governor. Not in 2000. "We started walking around the parking lot and saying hello to people," Cioffi says. "People would not make eye contact with him, and these were people who had supported him strongly in the past. Others would just turn their backs and walk away from him."

The ugliness continued. The fund-raising walk made its way toward downtown St. Albans; as Dean's party neared City Hall, the governor recognized a longtime supporter watching from the curb and went to give her a hug. As he did, Cioffi recalled, someone else, an elderly woman, approached the governor and said, "You fucking, queer-loving son of a bitch." Cioffi says Dean replied, "You should clean up your mouth, lady. You certainly didn't learn how to talk like that in Franklin County."

Against the advice of state police, Dean decided to stay in St. Albans that day and march in the Maple Festival parade. Dean told the troopers of his plans at the last minute. "They would have tried to talk him out of it," Cioffi says. "When we walked by, it was either dead silence or some people yelling something derogatory about civil unions. There were very few people applauding." Dean decided to follow his tradition of stopping at the American Legion and buying some of the maple syrup, candy and other products on display. "You have to walk by the bar to get to the open area," where the maple products were being sold, Cioffi says. There was more abuse. "When he walked in, some of the people started shouting obscenities."

By the end of the day, Dean knew he and the state had a problem. He and Cioffi talked about scheduling meetings at which the governor could hear from people, try to explain why the civil unions law was passed and try to allay widespread concerns about it. After discussing it with other advisers during the next few days, Dean settled on the forums as his strategy.

The first would be in St. Albans, on a hot, early-summer night in Cioffi's barn, a massive red structure built in 1848 by the family of John Gregory Smith, who served as Vermont's governor during the Civil War. About 100 chairs, borrowed from a church, were set up inside the barn; some 300 people showed up, lining up three and four deep along the walls. Guests entered through the driveway. "[Dean] greeted every person who came to the function that night. He stood there and shook their hands," Cioffi says.

After Cioffi introduced him, Dean "stood there and explained civil unions and said he understood that people felt strongly and differently — a lot of people — than he did, but that he felt he'd done the right thing. But he also asked for people to look at everything he'd done in his tenure as governor. . . . Then he opened it up to questions. People peppered him for almost an hour. It was right down to brass tacks. Folks were saying exactly what was on their minds: What he did was wrong; they never expected it of him. They lectured him about morality. One longtime Democratic woman in St. Albans got up and said she was really, really disappointed with him. She gave it right to him. We let every single person who had something to say say it. He just stood there and listened to everyone."

Finally, Harold Howrigan stood up. Howrigan was an elder

in one of the leading dairy-farming clans in Franklin County and was president of the St. Albans Co-operative Creamery, the linchpin of the area's farm economy. The Howrigans epitomized the conservative, Catholic but Democratic political tradition in that part of Vermont. Another member of the clan, former state senator Francis Howrigan, had stood on the floor of the Vermont Senate a decade earlier to denounce a bill protecting gay rights in housing and employment, saying it threatened to turn Vermont into a "society of corn-holers."

Cioffi quotes Harold Howrigan as follows: "'You know, I'm not for this civil unions issue, either. But this man has done a great job as governor. I think we need to look at him for everything that he's done and weigh that. When and if you do that, you're going to do what I'm going to do and vote for Howard Dean.'"[1]

Dean was in unfamiliar territory in 2000. He had reason to be confident in his past campaigns, even in 1998. He had run for four two-year terms since ascending to the governor's office in 1991. Vermont's Republicans for a while couldn't even find a candidate to run against Dean in 1992, in part because Dean had captured the broad middle of the political spectrum by keeping many of Richard Snelling's aides and sticking to his predecessor's program of deficit reduction. Finally, the GOP came up with John McClaughry, a state senator from Caledonia County in the Northeast Kingdom, and the owner of a political resume that included a stint as a policy adviser in the Reagan White House.

"I carried the [Republican] party flag, but I had no illusions about winning," says McClaughry, who describes himself as a libertarian. He says Dean succeeded in painting him as a "right-wing nut." McClaughry ended up with 23 percent of the vote.

Montpelier lawyer and school-choice advocate David F. Kelley had no better luck in 1994. Then it was John Gropper's turn. The businessman from the town of Rochester tried walking the length and breadth of Vermont as his main campaign shtick in 1996, which turned out to be better exercise than politics.

But the 2000 campaign was different for Dean.

A NATIONAL PLAYER

While his first three runs for governor were a breeze, Dean had a different sort of campaign already going on at the   national level. Almost immediately after Dean became governor, then-Colorado governor Roy Roemer, chairman of the National Governors Association (NGA), considered his potential and, beginning in about 1992, helped to groom Dean for leadership in that organization. "I was looking around to see where the new leadership might lie," says Roemer, who later served as superintendent of schools in Los Angeles. "He had very strong energy, a very high intellect. I was particularly struck by the forthrightness of the man and by his ethics."

B.J. Thornberry, a former aide to Roemer who went on to become executive director of the Democratic Governors' Association, says Dean made an unusually quick rise to the top rank of governors, becoming NGA chairman within three years of becoming governor of Vermont. He later led the Democratic Governors' Association and spent several years as recruitment chairman of that group.

Thornberry, who like Roemer is a Dean supporter, says it was unusual for someone to move from the chairmanship of the DGA to the lesser position of recruitment chairman, but Dean moved into that later role with relish. "He was very, very active. We could always count on him as a go-to governor," she says. Dean traveled the country, talking with state Democratic leaders, learning what he could about the political lay of the land, offering analyses of local situations and helping state parties get behind a particular candidate for governor. "He would not only do recruitment per se, but he would go in and really make an assessment of the field of candidates. . . . He told me from the get-go that we were going to get Oklahoma [in 2002], and we did it," Thornberry says. The election of Democrat Brad Henry in that normally conservative state "was one of the surprises, frankly, of 2002. But not for him, not for Governor Dean."

Dean's roles with the NGA and DGA helped him build the contacts for his own national campaign. Robert Rogan, then an

NGA staffer who later became a Dean aide in Vermont, says Dean's work with those groups showed the governor of tiny Vermont that he could win the respect of leaders around the country; it also allowed him to build confidence to eventually run for the White House.

The experience was of immense benefit to Dean, says Thornberry. Politics is best learned face-to-face, not on the phone. "You don't really know until you get out there and touch it and see it and hear it and smell it yourself," she says. Did Dean use his DGA position to plant the seeds for a national campaign? "I don't think that's the only reason. But look, it didn't hurt," she says. "The happy consequence for us was that he really threw himself into this role as recruitment chairman. I don't know when he first got the idea about running for president, or even if that was the motivation. But he did a superb job."

> "He had very strong energy, a very high intellect. I was particularly struck by the forthrightness of the man and by his ethics."
>
> *Roy Roemer,*
> *Former Governor of Colorado*

In 1999 Dean made his first, tentative move toward the presidency, floating a trial balloon about entering the primaries for the 2000 election. He dropped the idea quickly, however, after a meeting with Al Gore and after giving greater consideration to the demands a presidential race places on family.

FAMILY LIFE

One person who did not accompany Dean on his campaign trips around Vermont or to NGA meetings was his wife. Dr. Judith Steinberg remained behind, managing her medical practice in Shelburne and keeping track of the children, Anne and Paul. But Dean, too, took his family responsibilities seriously. The stories of Dean as devoted family man are legion.

Jane Williams, the longtime Dean aide and neighbor, says Dean and Steinberg were equal partners in child-rearing. The kids were in day care during the day when they were young, and their parents were loath to leave them with a babysitter in the evening, so they rarely went out. "We don't want to get a baby-sitter and leave them again," Williams quotes Judy as having once said. "We'd rather spend the evening with them — they're good company."

Occasionally, on school holidays, when Steinberg needed to see patients, Dean brought the kids with him to the office. Once before a press conference, press aide Sue Allen overheard him warning the children not to be alarmed if the press started grilling him with tough questions. Allen says the kids, often accompanied by a friend or two, would hang around the office, sometimes hitting the governor up for cash so they could skip off to the Statehouse cafeteria for a treat or buy ice cream in downtown Montpelier.

Even as the children became teenagers, Dean kept his social calendar open to be with family. "He's not a socializer in terms of hanging out with friends: It's work and family," says Attorney General and friend William Sorrell.

Both kids were soccer and hockey players, and Dean coached some of their youth hockey league teams — frequently rising for practices at 4 or 5 a.m. He was an exuberant fan — sometimes too much so. The governor's office was abuzz one morning with the story that Dean, at one of his kid's hockey games in Quebec, had received a stern warning from a referee for being too aggressive as a fan. "He was one of those guys who would really get into the game," Sorrell says with a laugh. "Sometimes he would be kind of embarrassed that he was as involved as he was."

When invited to speak at a political dinner, Dean would check his calendar and if the event conflicted with a child's sports event, he usually declined the invitation. If he agreed to appear at an evening event, particularly in southern Vermont, two or more hours from home, Dean often would ask to speak before dinner, and then skip the meal to be home before the kids' bedtime. He also used the governor's prerogative of designing his own schedule to his and his kids' advantage. For example, if a gubernatorial trip to St. Johnsbury in northeastern Vermont was in order, he would schedule it on a day when Paul or Anne had a hockey game there.

Dean had been an avid hiker, canoeist, skier and sailor. He has hiked the length of the Long Trail, a footpath that stretches from the Massachusetts border to Quebec along the spine of the Green Mountains. Judy and the kids joined him for parts of it. They also joined him in canoeing the length of Vermont's eastern border on the Connecticut River. Dean's home in Burlington is about a block from Lake Champlain, and the governor and the children often sailed on their small Sunfish sailboat that was a bit the worse for wear. "I always thought it was going to sink," Williams says.

The kids occasionally joined him on the campaign trail. Williams recalls one father-son appearance at a parade in Enosburg in northern Vermont. Seven or eight at the time, Paul stood engrossed in a book as Dean shook hands with passers-by. Paul kept track of his dad by touching him constantly with his elbow. "Paul wouldn't even take his eyes off the book, but he would realize when he didn't have his elbow against Howard, and he would just move," she says.

> Occasionally, on school holidays, when Judy Steinberg needed to see patients, Dean brought the kids with him to the office.

By 2003, Anne was away at Yale and Paul was in his junior year at Burlington High School, seemingly old enough to endure Dean's absences. But one night in the summer of 2003, Paul, described by classmates as bookish and friendly, got himself into trouble. He was picked up by police early one morning while acting as the driver for four of his high school hockey teammates who were burglarizing the Burlington Country Club to steal liquor. Paul admitted responsibility without making a formal guilty plea and entered a court diversion program requiring community service. Dean skipped two days of campaign events and flew home to Burlington. "Children do stupid things and this is one of them," Dean told a reporter. "I'm cutting short my next two days on the campaign trail to deal with a family problem that I consider to be a serious problem."

While the kids joined their father in parades and other public appearances, Judy stayed out of the limelight. An intensely shy person, dedicated to her medical practice, she never had to entertain or otherwise play the role of first lady during the 11 years her husband was governor. Vermont governors don't have a mansion, and that suited her just fine.

> Sartorially challenged, Howard Dean is often the target of comments about too-tight shirts and threadbare pants.

She granted her first-ever extensive interview in February 2003 to Christopher Graff, the correspondent in charge of the Associated Press bureau in Montpelier. She told Graff that she did not plan to campaign with her husband, but added: "If he really wants me someplace, I certainly would do it, but it would be between me and him."

She said that if he were elected president, she would hope to continue her minimalist approach to being first lady. She said she would move her professional life to Washington and practice medicine there.

But as low a profile as Judy has kept in her husband's public life, friends say she has been a huge influence on him privately. "Judy has given him the anchor, and the balance, he has needed," says David Wolk, Dean's friend, who is now president of one of Vermont's state colleges. "No one else gives him better advice. . . . She has kept him honest."

One thing she probably doesn't discuss with him, friends

say, are his clothes. Sartorially challenged, he is often the target of comments about too-tight shirts and threadbare pants.

Cioffi says that when he was economic development commissioner, he once accompanied Dean and other state officials to New York City to meet with financial services companies. Someone on Dean's staff pointed out that Dean's buttoned-down shirt was missing a collar button. Dean just unbuttoned the other button, Cioffi says. "About a week later I saw him at another thing, and he had the same shirt on," collar tips still unbuttoned.

A TEMPER

The agressiveness Dean displayed during his school days stayed with him, often erupting on his campaign trails. His opponents still complain about his combative style and tactics. They describe him as affable and full of good humor when things were going his way, but quick to anger when they weren't.

David Kelley says Dean is good at working a crowd. "He's got a lot of self-confidence. He speaks to people quickly, rapid-fire."

He also had, and has, a sense of humor. In one televised debate in 1994 against Kelley, Dean answered a question about farm policy by reminding viewers with a big smile that he had a "secret weapon" in the Agriculture Department: Kelley's father was his deputy commissioner.

But he could be petulant. Both McClaughry and Dwyer complain that he occasionally blindsided them inappropriately during their campaigns. McClaughry describes a "cattle show" of candidates for statewide office in 1992 at which each of about two dozen hopefuls gave a short statement about why he or she was running for office. He says he was astonished when Dean used his time to lash McClaughry's environmental record. McClaughry says Dean falsely accused him of opposing every environmental bill that had come out of the Senate Natural Resources Committee, on which the Republican had served. "Dean just started hammering on me," McClaughry says.

Dwyer took umbrage at the way Dean came after her in a

televised debate in September 2000 over her opposition to the civil unions law. In a tone both seething and dismissive, Dean asked her, "Where does tolerance fit into a Dwyer view?"

Dean's temper is palpable. "Whenever he's angry his neck swells out over his collar, his face gets red and he gets this funny look on his face," Dwyer says. "I always knew when he was getting to the point when he was about to blow."

She adds: "He's always attacking his opponents personally. How many people has he had to apologize to now [on the presidential] campaign trail?"

Dean's pique was not always directed at Republicans. During the 1994 campaign, Rivers, the liberal Democrat whose car was bashed by the property rights advocates, was speaking to a class at Springfield High School and criticizing Dean's handling of a health care reform bill. A local newspaper reporter was there and called Dean for comment. He told the reporter he hoped Rivers, even though a fellow Democrat, would not be re-elected to her state senate seat. It was a two-day story. The first day was Dean's comment. The next day, his apology.

A DIFFERENT DEAN IN 2000
But at the forums organized for him during the 2000 campaign, by all accounts, it was a different Dean, one more willing to take criticism from opponents than to dish it out.

Jane Costello of Rutland, who describes herself as an independent and a Dean backer, was one of those whom Dean asked to organize meetings of people who were upset with him. With help from people like her, Dean would visit living rooms or backyards across the state and deliver a few remarks and then open up the floor for questions and comments. "It was a forum for people to vent and express their concerns and to have a face-to-face dialogue with their governor," Costello says.

Another Dean supporter, Martha O'Connor, whose daughter Kate is one of Dean's closest aides, says the governor even asked her to gather a group of Republicans at their Brattleboro home, in the southeastern corner of Vermont, so he could hear their complaints.

In Arthur Ristau's backyard in Barre and in Frank Cioffi's barn in St. Albans, it was the conservative Democratic faithful who the governor wanted to meet.

It all paid off. On Election Day Polina received just shy of 10 percent of the vote; Dwyer received just shy of 40 percent and Dean received 50.45 percent, just enough to top the 50 percent margin that he needed to keep the election out of the Republican-controlled Legislature. Howard Dean had won his fifth two-year term as governor.

> But at the forums organized for him during the 2000 campaign, by all accounts, it was a different Howard Dean, one more willing to take criticism from opponents than to dish it out.

Dean won Barre by fewer than 200 votes. He won in the city of St. Albans and was able to stay close enough in surrounding Franklin County, picking up 43.3 percent against 45.9 percent for Dwyer countywide. Key to his victory was his big win in Chittenden County, where he received 58 percent of the vote.

SHARPENED SKILLS

Longtime Dean observers say his talks with Republicans and civil unions critics were not just an attempt to defuse the opposition but were also part of his effort to challenge himself and hone his thinking. Dean is both praised and criticized for his ability to absorb and make use of the political thinking that surrounds him. This tendency shows up strongly even in the slogans he uses. His claim to represent "the Democratic wing of the Democratic Party" is taken from the late senator Paul Wellstone, who was one of the party's leading liberals. His exhortation that it's "time to take our country back" is an echo from the Take Back Vermont movement that tried to defeat him in 2000.

What some see as political agility others paint in a less

kindly light. "Howard quite frankly has been blessedly unencumbered by deeply held principles," says Kelley. "He becomes the person he needs to be. He's very pragmatic."

As he launched his presidential bid, Dean saw that the left flank of the Democratic Party was wide open, with little strong advocacy for its positions from any of the declared or likely candidates, says Ken Dean (no relation), a longtime Democratic political operative in Vermont. So he went from being a governor who angered advocates for the poor with his budget cuts to the candidate representing "the Democratic wing of the Democratic Party."

As Dean cranked up his campaign in 2003, even critics from the group that has been most critical of him over the years — the liberal wing of the Vermont Democratic Party — were behind their former governor. "I have my differences with him, and I'm still very prepared to be disappointed if he ever gets anywhere," Rivers says. "But we helped make him into what he is. He's got a voice and part of that voice was created here."

Elizabeth Ready, a Burlington funeral director's daughter who grew up to be a state senator and Vermont's state auditor, offers a similar observation.

"He comes from Park Avenue, the Hamptons, Yale, and he comes up here and kind of falls into being governor," she says.

"Somebody like that has to earn my respect. I honestly believe he has learned a lot from Vermonters. He's governed in a place where there's a value to having principles. He almost has learned the value of fighting for things. It wouldn't ordinarily be my impulse to be proud of him. But he has taken a lot of the values of this place that is my place. He is speaking them to a nation that needs to hear them. You can ask the question, does he have any moral compass? I think he has gained a great deal from the people he has governed."

David Gram

Howard Dean's campaign manager, Joe Trippi, works the phone and computer at the Dean campaign headquarters in South Burlington.
(*Photo by John Pettitt, Dean for America*)

CHAPTER 9

Cyber Organizers Set a New Pace

Nicco Mele looks tired and harried, his dyed yellow hair flopping uncombed over his forehead. He's worried his computer network will collapse from the load of money streaming in online.

It's 2 p.m. It's the last day of June, the federal deadline for second-quarter fund raising, and Mele, Howard Dean's Webmaster, is watching the cyber cash pour in. In the small warren of office cubicles at Dean's headquarters in South Burlington, the mood is both frenetic and celebratory. As the Web team updates the fund-raising totals every half hour, the crowd of staffers — many look barely old enough to vote — cheers louder and louder. As the total passes $6.5 million, someone down the hall begins blasting on a paper party horn.

Mele seems oblivious to the mayhem. He's posted a picture of a baseball bat on the campaign Web site, with a caption asking people to "hit a home run" for Howard Dean. Hunched at a rickety table cluttered with paper and coffee cups, Mele, 26, squints into his computer screen. He clicks the mouse and sends yet another message to would-be contributors on Dean's e-mail list.

"I'm hoping this particular e-mail will just surge the

whole thing and we can make 750 grand today," he says. "That would be very, very cool."

If the server doesn't crash.

"That's what keeps me awake at night," Mele says.

The computers stay up. And by midnight, Mele's prediction turns out to be low: Dean collects $802,083 on the Internet that day alone. For the quarter he collects $7.6 million, including nearly $4 million online. No candidate has ever used the Internet to raise so much, so fast, and from so many people. Some 45,000 donors give online in this second quarter, with average contributions of $74.14. The computer-powered cash machine vaults Dean from the back of the pack to the top tier.

(In the third quarter, Dean raised even more — roughly $14.8 million, shattering President Clinton's $10.3 million record for a Democrat. The donations grew by more than $5 million in the final 10 days of that quarter.)

By any measure — the volume of cash collected, the number of online discussion groups, volunteer Web sites and Web searches — Dean has outpaced his rivals with the new tools of Internet politics.

The online bonanza is even more remarkable because it occurs just as many Washington insiders are ready to dismiss Dean's chances. On June 22, Tim Russert, the host of NBC's *Meet the Press,* grills Dean sharply on his record, the war in Iraq and national security issues. The candidate seems edgy, unprepared and occasionally evasive. His performance is universally panned in the next day's papers. But his supporters don't seem to care, or they have the opposite reaction. Donations spike that Sunday, launching the late-June run that sets campaign fundraising records.

A $508,000 Turkey Sandwich

The baseball bat that clobbered Dean's Democratic rivals swings again a month later for a fund-raising blitz staged to match a $2,000-a-plate dinner held in South Carolina by Vice President Dick Cheney. The Republican collects $300,000. Dean and his Web-powered bat raise $508,000.

The Cheney Challenge, as the Dean corps dubs the event, shows both the interactive force of the Internet and the mischievous virtuosity of campaign manager Joe Trippi. On the day of the vice president's fund-raiser, Trippi seizes on a suggestion from an online supporter that Dean eat at his desk and log on to chat with volunteers at the same time Cheney meets and greets his high-end donors. Minutes after the message comes in, Trippi orders a picture posted on the Web site of a grinning Dean munching a $3 turkey sandwich. The "Deaniacs" love it. More money cascades in.

Trippi, a veteran of six presidential campaigns, is dark-haired, brusque and intense. He seems to live on Diet Pepsi and adrenaline, and sometimes barks at staff members who don't jump to his orders fast enough. But Trippi, whose world-weary manner matches his years in the political trenches, gets evangelistic when discussing how the Internet is transforming politics. He says that as campaigns relied more and more on television to lure voters, the public dropped out.

"It's about $2,000 checks and TV — and bathing the masses in glowing stuff while they sit at home. That ain't democracy . . . because somewhere in that whole hurry-up for cash to get on TV, we left the people out. People stopped playing. They don't vote anymore," he says. "What the Internet has done is really simple. It's putting people back in the process."

Trippi has a prankster side and clearly likes to have fun at his rivals' expense. And despite his condemnation of TV advertising in contemporary presidential politics, he embraces the medium as a weapon in the campaign. He uses some of the money raised in the Cheney Challenge to put Dean TV ads on the air in Texas, just as President Bush flies home to his Crawford ranch for a 35-day vacation. The early ads are an in-your-face slam on the president; the audacious move generates more free publicity.

By summer's end, the campaign claims 385,000 supporters, with an Internet-based donor list of more than 100,000. With more than $10 million coming in, Trippi spends the money to launch TV ads in six early primary states. The move upends the primary race again and forces his rivals to reassess the timing of their own TV campaigns. Dean collects $1 million in four days — much from online donors — during a frenzied coast-to-coast late-summer tour.

The campaign blitz ends in New York City, and this time Webmaster Mele is not so lucky with his computer network. He has rigged a wireless system in a makeshift outdoor office in the city's Bryant Park to track the fund-raising finale and enter new voters into the Dean database. The baseball bat is on the Web site again as the campaign pushes to the $1 million goal. But as thousands log on around the country to cheer on the bat, the Dean Web log, or blog, crashes under the strain. Mele has to rush to a Kinko's down the street to update the totals.

ELECTRONIC GRASSROOTS CAMPAIGN

The Dean election effort has embraced all the tools of conventional modern politics, from direct mail to an impressive array of big-money donors from Hollywood. But more than any of his rivals, Dean has made the Internet the strategic focus of the campaign.

The Web team is the physical hub of the operation as well. The bloggers, Web designers and support staff work just outside Trippi's office door. The place has the caffeinated buzz of a late-night college cram session. Although the campaign shares its suburban office building with a stock brokerage firm, the Dean décor is definitely more dorm room than corporate. Movie posters and cartoons hang on the walls; pizza boxes and bag lunches compete for desk space. Some of the battered furniture came from a state government surplus sale. A donated red couch doubles as crash pad for the Web team's many all-nighters.

The connectivity of the Internet has brought not just money, but tens of thousands of volunteers. With online tools — streaming video ("DeanTV"), downloadable posters, fliers and even computer code for Web designers — Dean has spawned a nationwide community of cyber-organizers.

The Dean Web site makes it easy. Supporters can search by

ZIP code for Dean meetings; they can schedule an event and get the word out instantly on the Web. Donation forms, literature, sample letters and sign-up sheets are all available online. By late summer, volunteers had staged more than 3,600 Dean events, all arranged online.

These multitudes of campaign volunteers aren't just glued to their keyboards. They also knock on doors and canvass for votes. Trippi boasts that when the campaign e-mailed 481 people in Austin, Texas, last spring about an upcoming Dean rally, the message spread far beyond those with a mouse and a modem.

"Two hundred [of the 481] people had a meeting and decided they were going to leaflet the entire Latino community in Austin," he says. "City elections were also that Tuesday, and they decided they were going to assign each other, two to a polling place. And every person who voted in that city election got handed a leaflet saying Howard Dean is coming in three days. . . . We got to that park [in Austin]. There were 3,200 people there."

The *Wall Street Journal* seems to validate Trippi's claim when it compares the Dean Internet revolution to an earlier Web-driven uprising that transformed the business world. "At this point in the campaign, the Dean online operation is doing to political campaigns what Amazon.com did to retailing," the *Journal* reported in September. "For example, in the old-fashioned world of bricks-and-mortar politics, campaigns would send in a crew of advance people several days before a big event to drum up crowds. Dean staffers just send out e-mails, and thousands of supporters materialize."

> The connectivity of the Internet has brought not just money, but tens of thousands of volunteers.

Thousands of volunteers also connect monthly for in-person strategy sessions using a Web site called Meetup.com. In Vermont, the volunteers have turned to an old-fashioned form of communication as their latest form of political outreach. They've used pen and paper to introduce Dean to voters in New Hampshire, the state with the first-in-the-nation primary.

The Meetups and the Internet have brought a new generation into the campaign. Trippi likens the legions of young people who volunteer for Dean to the "kiddie corps" that energized the Democratic Party more than three decades ago.

"You've got to think of this a little bit like the old campaigns before television when we'd knock on doors. Who were the people actually banging on doors back then for Gene McCarthy and Bobby Kennedy? Kids, right? And whose doors were they knocking on?" Trippi answers the question. "Seniors, union people, you name it."

Crowds of young people turn out to hear Dean. But their online energy is not due to any love of technology on Dean's part. As governor, he earned a reputation as something of a Luddite. He rarely used a personal computer and didn't have a public state e-mail address. He seems astounded that he's become the campaign season's futuristic political strategist.

Dean credits Meetup.com with helping to bring in thousands of volunteers. On one of his first trips to Texas, a man introduced himself as his chief Texas coordinator. Dean says that when he got to Austin, he didn't even realize the campaign had a Texas field organizer.

"I said, 'You are?' He organized all of Texas — he's a former state legislator — through Meetup," Dean says.

MEETUP MAKES A DIFFERENCE

The concept behind Meetup is simple. The free service uses the Web to arrange real world, in-person gatherings. The discussion topics traverse the spectrum of hundreds of hobbies and interests, from knitting to pug breeding to politics. As long as five or more people say they want to meet to discuss a certain topic, the Meetup service schedules a session. The Meetups — Dean's are at 7 p.m. on the first Wednesday of the month — are usually held in restaurants, bars, cafés or coffeehouses. These businesses pay Meetup.com a fee for the customers the Web site brings in.

The Dean campaign also now pays Meetup $2,500 a month for its Web-based clearinghouse.

Dean staffers laugh that some of the rival campaigns originally dismissed the Meetups as barroom scenes from *Star Wars*. But Trippi realized early on its potential for political organizing. Others in the organization were skeptical. When he first asked the tech staffers to put a link to Meetup.com on the Dean homepage, they resisted. "From the first day I got here, I wanted that site linked," he says. It took him a week to get it operating, much longer than he had hoped.

> "Who were the people actually banging on doors back then for Gene McCarthy and Bobby Kennedy? Kids, right?"
>
> *Joe Trippi,*
> *Campaign Manager*

Meetup turned out to be a perfect match for Dean. By early September, 109,000 people had signed up through the Web service to continue the grassroots campaign. Dean's closest Meetup rivals, Rep. Dennis Kucinich of Ohio and former NATO Commander Wesley Clark, each had around 12,000 Meetup volunteers.

The August Meetup in Montpelier had to move out of a downtown bar and into a larger church basement. Sixty-seven people showed up, about three times as many as organizers expected.

It's muggy in the basement, and an overhead fan merely stirs the humidity as the new arrivals introduce themselves and pull metal chairs up to folding tables. The age of the crowd seems to run from 18 to 80. Greg Hysman, the unpaid coordinator of Dean's campaign in the county, makes a plea for volunteers to go to New Hampshire the next weekend to canvass door-to-door for votes. A tall, elderly man from the farming town of Danville tells how he set up a Dean booth at a county fair. "We had a notary there to sign up new voters," he says. "There are so many disillusioned voters out there, and this campaign is bringing them in right along."

Andrea Stander, a Dean volunteer organizer, gives a pep talk on the importance of using e-mail lists to spread the word. "That's what's making this work. It's people to people. It's friend to friend, relative to relative," says Stander. "And if you don't do e-mail, get a bunch of Vermont postcards and send them out."

Tom Luce, a veteran Democratic Party activist from Barre, says at the Meetup that e-mail and the Internet transformed his work in political organizing. "I think Dean has an edge on this. You don't see anybody else doing it that way. And it's real. It's not just cyberspace," Luce says. "I mean, the people I organize are real people who've never been organized before. This is a way they can get involved."

DEAN MEETS UP

A month later in Santa Fe, New Mexico, the Meetup crowd is bigger and more boisterous. Dean, who has flown in for a Democratic Party debate, is scheduled to stop by. An hour before the 7 p.m. start, about 200 people are packed into the Tribes Coffeehouse in the city's historic downtown. Organizers keep careful count because the fire code prohibits more than 220 inside. When the maximum is reached, they rig up a public address system for the overflow gathered in a covered courtyard.

Although New Mexico is 42 percent Hispanic, the Santa Fe Meetup attracts an almost all-white audience. Aging hipsters and young Iraq-war opponents seem to make up the mix. The homogeneous crowd shows that while Dean has huge support among liberals and the computer literate, he needs to work hard to reach the other side of the digital divide.

"First of all, most of us don't have computers," says Rudy Clark, a Democrat, Hispanic and member of New Mexico's Human Rights Commission who is waiting to hear Dean. "Remember, who has computers?" she says. "The more affluent members of society. Who are Hispanics? They usually wash the dishes."

Clark says the Internet works well to get a white crowd out to see the candidate. But she says Dean needs more traditional tactics, including key endorsements, to really reach many Hispanic voters.

"For Dean to be successful he needs to have a spokesperson in this state who is Hispanic and speaks Spanish and does commercials for him or with him," she says. "That's the dynamic. It's always been the dynamic in this part of the country."

At about 7:20, the crowd parts as if for a prizefighter on the way to the ring. Dean breezes in with his entourage and a special guest. Kathy Padfield, a mental health worker from Denver, is the 100,000th person to sign up for a Dean Meetup. The campaign has flown her down from Colorado for the event. She beams from the makeshift stage as Dean introduces her.

Dean thanks the throng and then gives his doctor's orders: Each one of you, he says, must sign up at least five more people for the e-mail list.

"We want to get to 450,000 e-mails by the end of this month. We want to get to a million by the end of the year. The only way we can beat George Bush is to get a couple million people to the polls who haven't voted before," he says. "And this time the person with the most votes is going to win."

Dean looks decidedly un-Santa Fe. While most of the men are wearing faded denim, he's very East Coast, dressed in a charcoal suit and red tie. But he's relaxed and completely on his game. "This is going to work," he says. "Now, many of you know what my policies are so I won't give my stump speech."

But of course he does, segueing effortlessly through the themes he's sounded now for over a year. He calls for a foreign policy that "reflects America's values," a balanced budget that doesn't squander the nation's future, health care for all, no more tax breaks "for Ken Lay and the boys."

He speaks for 18 minutes without notes, pausing only occasionally to mop his brow. Then he takes questions for 15 minutes. And this is when it's clear the man is a marathon runner, ready with the physical stamina to handle the punishing pace of a non-stop, two-year campaign.

The chronic lack of sleep, bad food, endless forced smiles — none of it shows as he hits his stride in Santa Fe.

Indeed, earlier in the afternoon he delivered much the same speech at a private fund-raiser that netted $50,000. Yet he recites every word as if it was spontaneously conceived and fresh on his tongue. He projects a command of the issues and connects with a mixture of humor and red meat rhetoric.

Dean doesn't share any biographical or confessional detail in this stump speech. He rarely talks about his past, except for his experience as governor. He doesn't offer touchstones from his life or tell anyone he feels their pain. Instead, he reels in the audience by evoking a shared vision of a better America. He starts by recalling the upheaval in the country at the end of the 1960s.

A campaign staffer grabs a bite to eat while working on his laptop at the Dean campaign headquarters in South Burlington. (Times-Argus *Photo by Jeb Wallace-Brodeur*)

"I remember when I was about 21 years old, the civil rights movement was coming to an end, and it was a terrible time for America in some ways because Martin Luther King had been killed, Bobby Kennedy had been killed," he says.

"Enormous sacrifice had been made. Many others had gone to Mississippi and Alabama and been murdered there for their belief in equality for all Americans.

"But it was a great, heady time in many ways because we believed at the end of that time that we were all in this together, that it wasn't enough for us to want good schools in Vermont and for you to want good schools in Santa Fe. That you had responsibility as an American citizen and that I had one too —

that we have good schools in Santa Fe and in Vermont and also in Mississippi and Alabama and in Oakland, California, too."

The Bush administration, Dean says, has lost the respect of allies and lost 3 million jobs. "But the biggest loss we've had is our sense of community, our sense that we're all in this together." He accuses Bush of dividing the country by race, by gender, class and sexual orientation.

"I want a president that can appeal to the best in us, not the worst in us. . . . I want to appeal to the very best in America, to our ideals, to the notion that we're all in this together."

This is the speech's core message. Dean artfully turns the focus from himself — a politician searching for votes — to the audience, idealistic and eager for change. "What I want is a government and a country that is based on hope again and not fear," he says. "We can do better than this." When he delivers his signature line — "you have the power" — the crowd breaks out cheering.

Dean closes with a plea for everyone to get back online and recruit more volunteers. "We need help in calling people. We need you to reach out to at least five people," he says. "We need to do this in Albuquerque. We need to do this in White Sands. We need to do this all over New Mexico."

THE MEDIUM AND THE MESSAGE
Over the next four days, 9,000 people sign up over the Internet, continuing an online onslaught that has stunned other Democrats and heartened those who deplore the role of big money in politics.

Carol Darr, who was general counsel to the National Democratic Committee in 1992 and later worked in the Clinton administration's Commerce Department, sees Dean's use of the Internet as a sea change that has the potential to radically reform presidential politics.

"I think the Internet in this election has transformed everything," she says.

For decades, she continues, campaigns were fueled by wealthy donors — limited for the past three decades to $1,000 contributions per person — who demand access and influence for their money.

"Nobody thought you could do it any other way," she says. "And Howard Dean is showing that there is another way to do it."

Darr, who now directs George Washington University's Institute for Politics, Democracy and the Internet, says Dean's online campaign targeting small-scale donors has encouraged participation from people who had never been involved in politics.

"And small money is clean money," she says. "In presidential campaigns you've got a disturbing 28-year trend, since the post-Watergate reforms, that presidential campaigns are funded by maxed-out donors. And for the first time with Dean, you have the possibility that somebody actually might win the nomination based on small contributions."

The small donors can also be tapped again and again before they reach the $1,000 limit. And by giving in small amounts, they can fully leverage federal matching funds, which provide a dollar-for-dollar match for the first $250 from each donor.

> There's another, inherently pragmatic advantage to Internet fund raising: It's cheap. The overhead for e-mail is very low compared with direct mail or lavish fund-raising dinners.

There's another, inherently pragmatic advantage to Internet fund raising: It's cheap. The overhead for e-mail is very low compared with direct mail or lavish fund-raising dinners. Dean, of course, is still using all the fundraising tools, including private meetings at country clubs and in Hollywood.

Darr says Dean has broken through with the Internet the same way that Franklin D. Roosevelt revolutionized the use of radio and John F. Kennedy harnessed television. While other campaigns have slick Web sites and aggressive fund raising, Dean's success is due to both the medium and the message, she says. The Vermonter's candidacy — from his early opposition to the war with Iraq to his direct challenge to other Democrats — has energized a base that then organized online. But it first needed a compelling message to work, she says.

"It's partly the technology. But I think the thing that people are missing is the fact that he's a high-touch candidate, more than a high-tech candidate," Darr says. "The radio benefits candidates whose voice you want in your living room. Television benefits candidates who have a sense of presence, who are good-looking and who have the money to afford expensive television commercials. The Internet is different because it is interactive. And that's just a fancy way of saying that it allows a two-way conversation between candidates and citizens."

ORGANIZING CHAOS

Actually, in this campaign they seem to type more than they talk. The Dean blog — an ongoing Web journal — brims with entries from the campaign trail. Dean occasionally logs on to thank volunteers. Supporters from all over the country keep a running dialogue about issues, press coverage and ideas.

The official blog, and the dozens of local blogs and unofficial Web sites, form a giant feedback loop for the campaign. At best, the hundreds of daily posts are an immense national conversation that shares issues and ideas. At their worst, they devolve into simple partisan cheerleading. Often, a thread will discuss strategy questions that were once the sole province of professional staff: how to bring African-Americans into the campaign, for example, or how hard to hit Democratic rivals in an upcoming debate. Bloggers are fiercely protective of their candidate, but sometimes critical. After a September debate in New Mexico, the online fans pleaded with the campaign to improve Dean's style.

"I'd like to see him slow it down, articulate the facts, deliver with a more conversational feel rather than like he's at a rally," a blogger named Kim wrote. "I hate to make this comparison, but I have to admit, Kerry had a good smooth manner at this last debate and I think that our guy should break down and get some coaching so he can deliver his amazing messages in the best and most articulate way."

The culture of the Internet is fast, sometimes fickle, but above all decentralized. Dedicated users take pride in the non-hierarchical — actually anarchical — nature of the Net. Ideas whip back and forth in real time. In theory, no one commands so everyone holds some control.

This is the danger and the opportunity for a campaign that has embraced the Internet. Manager Trippi says it's an "open source" organization, a metaphor borrowed from the software world. Instead of the headquarters owning the code, the campaign invites the grassroots to tinker, invent and write their own programs. Ideas and strategy have poured in from the edges to become cornerstones of the campaign. The slogan "People-Powered Howard" became a campaign mantra after someone suggested it online. The original idea to use Meetup.com to organize volunteers came from an unofficial Dean Web log, Trippi says.

The danger comes if the unsanctioned campaign goes over the line. A group of Dean supporters, who've dubbed themselves the Dean Defense Forces, have organized themselves to act as media watchdogs. When Defense Forces members see a media report they consider inaccurate, they bombard the reporter or producer with critical e-mails. The technique hasn't endeared itself to those on the receiving end.

After Dotty Lynch, CBS's senior political editor, criticized Dean's foreign policy in her Web column, *Political Points,* she found herself under fire from the Defense Forces.

"They were all rather insulting: 'Why don't you do your research?'" Lynch told Howard Kurtz, the media columnist for the *Washington Post.* "When anything's orchestrated, you sort of smell a rat."

Trippi, the center of this wildly spinning Internet cyclone, isn't worried about these unscripted messages damaging the campaign. But, he says, as a manager the hardest thing about the campaign's Internet evolution is to let it drive itself.

"That's one of the reasons none of the other campaigns can get it going. This isn't about what their Web sites are like or how interactive their Web site is," Trippi says. "You have to let go. And if you can't let go, you will suffocate the Net roots. So the hardest thing for me . . . as somebody who intellectually understands I have to let go, but who is 47 years old and has never been able to let go of anything in my life . . . is to let go of the wheel."

> With Howard Dean, Joe Trippi found a candidate who knew he didn't have a chance unless he ran a bold, innovative campaign.

Trippi's political experience straddles both the new technology and the old pavement-pounding political techniques. He labored for years as a field organizer and political strategist, working for Gary Hart, Walter Mondale and Dick Gephardt. His firm, Trippi, McMahon and Squier, also consulted for a slew of other office-seekers, including Howard Dean in his gubernatorial campaigns. But Trippi also went to school in Silicon Valley. He's a computer geek and has advised high-tech firms, including Progeny Linux Systems, a company that specializes in open-source computer operating systems.

With Dean, Trippi found a candidate who knew he didn't have a chance unless he ran a bold, innovative campaign. Trippi's advice to Dean early on was counterintuitive but effective. "The only way we can win," he says he told Dean, "is to act like we have nothing to lose." It's a high-wire strategy. But with almost every move, from his early opposition to the Iraq war to his foray into online organizing to his early TV ad campaign, Dean has outflanked his opposition.

Trippi says Dean came to the Internet not even knowing what a blog was, but he learned fast. Soon he was blogging on the campaign's site and on a site maintained by Larry Lessig, a law professor in San Francisco and respected Internet visionary.

"He wasn't very good at it," Trippi says. "In fact, some of the people who commented said, 'I was worried that they were going to ghostwrite some of this stuff, but this looks like it was written by an automaton.' I commented back: 'Don't you think if we were ghostwriting this stuff, it would be better written than this?'"

BUILDING THE WEB TEAM

Dean may not be an expert blogger, but he's an extremely savvy and instinctive politician. The serendipity that has so far blessed his political career has carried through to the evolution of his Internet organizing.

Trippi came to the campaign in early 2003 after the first manager quit. With less than $157,000 in the bank and seven people on staff, he says, the strategy was simple: Focus on fund raising, the Internet and the early-decision states of Iowa and New Hampshire.

Trippi knew he wanted to improve the campaign's rudimentary Web presence. The first Web site was not interactive and didn't allow people to donate online. The site was so bad, says Trippi, that unofficial Web sites — those created by Dean supporters on their own — were fielding calls from national reporters looking for the real campaign.

The catalyst came in February 2003 when a young political activist named Mathew Gross wandered into Trippi's office. The 31-year-old writer and former rock band drummer was living in Moab, Utah. He was a frequent contributor to a Web blog called MyDD.com (the initials stand for My Due Diligence, an insider's daily journal on politics). Gross had followed the growing chatter about Dean and thought the Democrat could do well in the inter-mountain West, particularly because of his states'-rights stance on gun control. And like many disaffected Democrats, Gross was inspired by Dean's sharp questions on the Iraq war. He felt Dean had the potential to lead Democrats back from the wilderness they had been wandering in since the midterm congressional election defeats of 2002.

Gross had one major complaint. Dean's Web presence was

horrible. "The last place I would go online in January or February for information about Howard Dean was the Dean For America Web site," he says.

Gross had planned to volunteer at Dean headquarters for a week or two after he visited his parents in New Hampshire. In Burlington, he sidled past the reception desk and made it to Trippi's office. He handed over a memo about the Internet's potential to organize voters.

Trippi listened distractedly to the pitch, until Gross mentioned that he wrote for MyDD.com. Trippi knew the blog and had followed the building chatter about Dean.

"He sort of sat up straight in his chair and looked at me," Gross recalls. "He said: 'Go back to Utah. Get your stuff. You're hired.'"

In a few hours, Gross had the first official Dean blog up on the Internet. They named it Call to Action. Trippi remembers that Web site the way some people cherish memories of their first car. It was creaky, somewhat ugly, but it got them going.

But Trippi also remembers its shortcomings. "[Gross] is a great blogger, but he had come here without any clothes. It actually made me question his thought process. He didn't pack anything. And now he had to go straight home to get all his stuff. . . . I said, 'You can have the job, but before tomorrow you've got to put the Call to Action blog up.' He got it done in two hours, and it didn't look great."

Nicco Mele, who had worked as Webmaster for Common Cause, a liberal group based in Washington, was hired as the Dean Webmaster. Zephyr Teachout, a 31-year-old lawyer, also joined the blog squad as "director of Internet outreach."

The first blog didn't have a comment section to allow supporters to post their feedback. Trippi notes with competitive chagrin that Gary Hart, the former Colorado senator, was the first to launch an interactive presidential campaign blog last year when he was considering running for president.

But Trippi credits Hart with teaching him in the 1980s some fundamentals of political organizing, techniques that have carried over to the Internet.

Hart "believed in something called concentric circle organizing," Trippi says. "You drop a rock in the water and the waves ripple out. The theory of how he organized his presidential campaign in 1984 was to go someplace, basically drop a rock in the water in Iowa City, Iowa, and leave. And then let the ripples of those people working together basically create the campaign. It occurred to us that the Internet was concentric circle organizing on steroids."

The Internet has not replaced the essentials of street campaigning; it's just put everything on warp speed, Trippi says. For example, early in the summer the Dean campaign offered tailor-made posters that supporters could download from the Web site. There were posters for all 50 states. But soon someone e-mailed from Puerto Rico and pointed out that Puerto Rico also votes for president and participates in the delegate selection process.

> Joe Trippi says the Internet has moved campaigns from an era of television dominance to a time when citizens can get involved again.

The campaign instantly created a "Puerto Rico for Dean" poster.

"And that's what the Net does. It doesn't change the fact that you have a lot of signs out there," Trippi says. "It's just now there's [greater] ability to have people tell you where the holes are in your campaign and for you to plug them."

John McCain in 2000 used the Web successfully for fund raising. But Trippi says the Internet is more mature now and was ripe for a campaign that understands its potential.

"Millions of Americans have bought something on Amazon. They've traded something on eBay or bought a piece of music. They are comfortable putting their credit card on the Net in that box and clicking 'submit,'" he says.

Trippi isn't modest about what he thinks the campaign has achieved. He says the Internet has moved campaigns from an era of television dominance to a time when citizens can get involved again.

"The Kennedy-Nixon debate should have been a big signal to a lot of people that television was about to radically change our politics," he says. "Eight days in June I think will be seen sometime in the future as the day people should have realized that the Internet was going to radically change America's politics. The difference was the first revolution ended up taking people out of the process. This one is putting people back in."

John Dillon

Presidential hopeful Howard Dean makes
a point while speaking to a crowd
on September 23, 2003,
at Copley Square in Boston.
(AP Photo by Olivia Nisbet)

CHAPTER 10

What Kind of President?

Howard Dean likes Harry Truman. He also likes Jimmy Carter, Martin Luther King Jr., John F. Kennedy, even Teddy Roosevelt when it comes to conservation. But none of them gets as much attention from Dean as does the 33rd president.

On domestic policy, Dean pledges to "fulfill Harry Truman's dream of health care for all Americans," and when it comes to foreign affairs, he cites as a model Truman's Point Four program aimed at providing technological skills and equipment to poor nations.

"Harry Truman believed that a world in which even the poorest and most desperate had grounds for hope would be a world in which our own children could grow up in security and peace," Dean says. Truman may come as close as anyone to being Dean's role model.

"I admire him a lot," Dean says in an interview. "There are similarities between us. We're both plainspoken. He took some really tough positions. The integration of the armed forces was an extraordinary position at the time. So was recalling General MacArthur," the popular if insubordinate war hero Truman removed from command during the Korean War in 1951.

No wonder Truman is a Dean hero. Vice President Truman became president the way Lt. Gov. Dean became governor, when his predecessor died unexpectedly. Dean sees himself as a politician tough enough to do what he thinks is right, whether or not it's popular, just as Truman did.

So would President Dean be like President Truman?

Well, maybe he would be more like a combination of President Truman and President Eisenhower.

An updated version of that combination, to be sure. Neither Eisenhower nor Truman had to deal with gay rights, international terrorism or the controversy over downloading free music on campus computers. But they brought attitudes and values to the job that Dean seems to share.

As a good Democrat, Dean does not often mention Ike's name. But no one should be surprised if he starts. Praising a president from the other party makes a candidate seem fairminded, and in this case, the reference would not be phony. There is a lot of Eisenhower in Dean.

Truman was president when Howard Dean was born and Eisenhower is the first president Howard Dean can remember. Like both of them, Dean is an old-fashioned guy — unpretentious, unadorned, frugal, blunt. For 11 years, Dean governed Vermont rather like an Eisenhower Republican, and some of the positions he takes on the campaign trail sound downright "Eisenhowsish," as the lyricist Yip Harburg put it.

"I balance budgets," Dean says. "No Republican president has balanced the budget in 34 years in this country. You can't trust them with your money."

Change "Republican" to "Democratic," and that could have been a sound bite from any Republican campaign of a generation ago, when Republicans boasted of their prudence and assailed Democrats for their sloppiness with the taxpayer's dollar. In those days, Republicans were the budget balancers, and, as it happens, Howard Dean was growing up in a Republican household.

Vestiges of Republicanism remain. Just as Ronald Reagan, raised a New Deal Democrat, never quite stopped being what his political strategists called a "cultural Democrat," Dean retains some of the political attitudes of his upbringing. Dean's father was a rather conservative Republican, but the political milieu surrounding young Howard as he grew up amid the New York financial community was dominated by the centrist Republicanism of Gov. Nelson Rockefeller — fiscally conservative but socially liberal.

It isn't that Dean is anything but a confirmed Democrat. In fact, on a standard list of issues, Dean is indistinguishable from his Democratic opponents. He is against privatizing Social Security, means-testing Medicare, drilling in the Arctic National Wildlife Refuge, public subsidies for private schools, and Bush's air-quality and forestry policies. He is for a Medicare-based prescription drug plan for seniors, a woman's right to choose an abortion, tougher fuel-efficiency requirements for automobiles, Bill Clinton's Roadless Area plan for the national forests, and restoring tighter FCC rules on media ownership.

Still, he clings to a few traditional Republican instincts. Deficit spending, high taxes and aggressive social engineering are bad; balanced budgets, big business and stiff sentences for criminal offenders are good. As governor, he cut taxes, balanced the budget, supported the electric utility industry, defended corporate interests and — like Ike — got into more squabbles with the far-out wing of his own party than with the opposition.

Even in two areas where Dean takes what is generally considered a liberal stance — civil rights and civil liberties — it is a liberalism consistent with his upbringing during an era when moderate Republicans such as Rockefeller and Chief Justice Earl Warren led the fight for integration, and when Northeastern Republicans were among the strongest supporters of freedom of expression and personal privacy.

Dean supports affirmative action, arguing that it is needed to offset what he calls a sweeping "unconscious bias" to prefer one's own. He tells the story of asking his chief of staff, a woman, if she could hire a man for a position on his predominantly female staff, only to be told, "You know, it's really hard to find a qualified man."

"Everybody does it," says Dean. "It's not just 54-year-old white guys like me who want to hire people like myself."

And he has been sharply critical of some provisions of the post–September 11 USA Patriot Act and Attorney General John Ashcroft's vigorous enforcement of it.

"After September 11, the Ashcroft Justice Department took advantage of the climate of fear and adopted a series of anti-terror tactics that go far beyond protecting our country and [that] erode the rights of average Americans," Dean says. "We should be rolling these back. As president, I will lead the war on terror in a way that protects civil rights and civil liberties as well as our safety."

A MODERATE MIX

If Dean becomes president, then the policies he would propose and execute would most likely resemble an ideological hybrid, a mix of moderate Republican and mainstream Democratic, with a more energetically liberal approach on a few issues.

That is assuming, of course, that his campaign speeches and his policies as governor are accurate guides to what kind of a president he would be. There is a school of thought that insists they signify nothing, that politicians will "say anything to get elected" and afterward do as they wish, or as directed by the powerful interests that support and finance them.

There is some evidence to justify this cynicism. Jimmy Carter promised to reform the tax code. Ronald Reagan said he would balance the budget. George H.W. Bush insisted he would not raise taxes. Bill Clinton vowed a tax cut for the middle class, and George W. Bush assured America he would pursue a humble foreign policy that would eschew "nation building." They didn't.

But every one of them led the country generally in the direction their campaigns indicated. Reagan cut taxes and spent more on the military, just as he said he would. Bush pére promised a "kinder and gentler" Reaganism and delivered a conservative administration leavened by the Americans with Disabilities Act and a stronger Clean Air Act. Clinton raised taxes on the wealthiest and expanded health care coverage, as promised. George W. Bush said he would cut taxes and expand petroleum production, and he has. Campaign promises are wish lists, only some of which presidents can accomplish. But their wishes point the way they want to go.

At any rate, the only way the citizen can try to assess how a presidential hopeful will govern is to listen to what the candidate says, examine how he or she performed in other positions, observe which interest groups support him, and consider with whom he has associated and who influences him.

Here Howard Dean is something of an enigma. He doesn't have many political associations. Both as a person and as a politician Dean has been not exactly a loner, but a bit standoffish, the antithesis of the back-slapping, howz-the-wife-and-kids pol. As governor, he was active in the National Governors Association, earning enough respect of his peers to become its chairman. But not one of the Democratic governors who served with him rushed to endorse his candidacy.

> If Howard Dean becomes president, then, the policies he would propose and execute would most likely resemble an ideological hybrid, a mix of moderate Republican and mainstream Democratic, with a more energetically liberal approach on a few issues.

Nor has he any long-standing connections with the leaders of Democratic-leaning interest groups. As a presidential candidate, he has courted the leaders of organized labor, most of whom he hardly knew. Though he is considered a friend of the environment, he has not been a close friend of the environmentalists, and aside from Vermont's congressional delegation, there is hardly a senator or representative with whom he has gone to lunch. He has gotten the backing of some gay and lesbian political organizations, grateful for his support of the civil unions law in 2000. But these are recent alliances.

Over the years, Dean has relied considerably on the advice of three Vermonters, ranging from a somewhat conservative Republican to a rather liberal Democrat. The Republican is Harlan Sylvester, the senior executive at Salomon Smith Barney in Burlington, who was Dean's top economic adviser when he was governor and who went on to advise Dean's successor, a Republican. The liberal Democrat is Peter Welch of White River Junction, the majority leader of the state Senate. In between, ideologically speaking, is Wayne Granquist, a businessman like Sylvester (he used to own a couple of Vermont ski areas), but a Democrat who was a senior official in the Office of Management and Budget under President Jimmy Carter. Granquist is now on the Dean campaign's issue staff.

Dean also remains close to his brother William, a businessman who converted from Republican to Democrat in May 2003 to support his brother's campaign.

As a candidate, Dean has reached out to new advisers without apparent regard to ideology. One is liberal economist James K. Galbraith of the University of Texas, who summers in Vermont. Another is Maya MacGuineas, a centrist fiscal expert associated with the non-partisan New America Institute.

He has also consulted with former EPA director Carol Browner, former Carter adviser Gene Eidenberg, former Clinton domestic affairs chief Gene Sperling and scholars from the centrist-to-liberal Brookings Institution, all of whom are best placed in the Democratic center.

GUN RIGHTS, GAY RIGHTS

To understand Dean's ideological orneriness, simply consider his positions on gun control, where he seems as far to the right as a Democrat gets, and gay rights, where he has been placed on the far left thanks to Vermont's civil unions law. A closer examination reveals that he is neither all that conservative on the one nor radical on the other.

"I'm not a big gun control guy," Dean said in a New Hampshire radio interview in July. "Background checks should be applied to gun shows, but I don't believe you ought to have a national gun control bill. Whatever you want in New Hampshire you can have. Then if you want a whole lot more because you're from Massachusetts or New Jersey, then you should have a whole lot more. Don't tell us in Vermont and Montana what we should do about guns. . . . Why can't the states decide for themselves?"

This pleases the National Rifle Association, though it might not go over too well in Maryland, where gun control laws are strict but where a sniper killed six people in 2003 with a gun bought in Washington state. And it displeases the leading gun control lobby, the Brady Center to Prevent Gun Violence, whose president, Michael Barnes, said, "Electing Howard Dean president would not be a step forward toward making our children and our communities safer from gun violence. We intend to make sure Americans know that."

> To understand Howard Dean's ideological orneriness, simply consider his positions on gun control, where he seems as far to the right as a Democrat gets, and gay rights, where he has been placed on the far left thanks to Vermont's civil unions law.

But like the Brady Center and unlike the NRA, Dean favors extending the ban on assault rifles and closing the "gun-show" loophole in the Brady Act. Like the gun control lobby and unlike the NRA, he opposes a bill granting the gun industry immunity from almost all lawsuits.

He opposes only a nationwide licensing and registration plan. But there is no such plan. Gun control advocates have no intention of urging Congress to pass a comprehensive gun control law. In other words, Dean agrees with the gun control forces on all of their active proposals except one: limiting purchasers to one firearm a month. But that isn't going anywhere either.

As to gay rights, the civil unions law was not Howard Dean's idea. It was all but forced on Dean and the state legislature by the state Supreme Court, which ruled that depriving same-sex couples of the privileges granted to married couples violated the Vermont Constitution.

In an unusual ruling, the court said the state could either allow homosexual marriage or create another mechanism giving same-sex couples the same inheritance, insurance, adoption and joint ownership advantages enjoyed by married couples. State officials faced a stark choice: Comply or lead a divisive campaign to overturn the court's decision.

They chose compliance, and within that choice opted for the moderate alternative: equal treatment, but not same-sex marriage. Indeed, the law passed in 2000 declares that only a man and a woman may marry.

Dean does not support gay marriage. He favors equal rights, he says, including replacing the military's "don't ask, don't tell" policy with full equality for gay recruits and giving federal employees the right to name same-sex partners as insurance beneficiaries. Nor would he propose a nationwide civil unions law. On gay rights and gun rights, Howard Dean is for states' rights.

TAX POLICY

Republicans and some Democrats also try to paint Dean as an ultra-liberal over taxes. Dean wants to rescind all of President Bush's tax cuts. Republicans say that makes him a "high-tax liberal," and some of his Democratic opponents criticize him for wanting to annul even the Bush tax cuts for low- and middle-income earners.

But here Dean is less the income-redistributing populist than the Democrats who want to raise taxes only on the highest-income earners. Dean, who abolished Vermont's income tax surcharge on the wealthy, has never believed in soaking the rich.

"The bottom line is this," he says. "What Democrats can't afford to do is what Democrats have done in the past, promise everything to everybody. So I guess my retort is, if you're not in favor of getting rid of all the Bush tax cuts, tell me what you don't want to do. But don't go and tell us you're going to balance the budget, promise them everything, because people don't believe that from politicians anymore."

What Dean, the New Deal Democrat, is telling middle-income Americans is that most of them would be better off paying a little more in taxes to get a stronger economy and more in public services. He is effectively responding to an old Republican question most Democrats have feared to answer: Who can spend your money better — you or the government? Dean is saying that for everyone but the wealthy, the answer may well be the government — that solvent Social Security and Medicare systems, a prescription drug plan for the elderly, clean air and water, safe parks and playgrounds, and other services for the middle class are worth more to most people than the $650 a year, which is the average tax saving for people in the middle of the income spectrum. (That is according to Robert McIntyre of Citizens for Tax Justice, a liberal organization whose numbers are accepted across the ideological spectrum.)

At the same time, Dean, the Eisenhower Republican, argues that keeping the budget in balance will lead to stronger economic growth, hence more and better jobs. "Most Americans would be happy to pay the taxes they paid under Bill Clinton if they could have the kind of economy they had under Bill Clinton," he says repeatedly. And Dean, the moderate, says that's as far as he wants to go. After getting back to the Clinton-era tax rates, he'd oppose new increases.

But rare indeed is the politician who can resist offering some kind of tax cut to the venerated middle-income American, and Howard Dean is not immune from this temptation. For a while, late in the summer of 2003, he and his aides played with the notion of restoring the Clinton-era tax rates to everyone, but throwing in a credit on Social Security and Medicare payroll taxes for everyone in the lower- and middle-income brackets.

It might have been both good politics and good economics, but then the August Congressional Budget Office numbers came out, revealing that the Iraq war costs and the long-term deficit outlook were worse than expected. Dean resisted the temptation after all, at least until the budget outlook improves. He will continue to talk about tax fairness, his campaign advisers say. But as of the fall in 2003, he had decided to hold off on middle-class tax breaks.

> "One reason I am running for president is to restore the ideal of the American community."
>
> Howard Dean,
> 2003 Campaign

There is another reason for Dean's insistence that everyone contribute to the federal treasury. It supports his notion that everyone is responsible for everyone else, a sense of national community that Dean talks about almost every time he speaks to voters. This communitarian point of view is less a specific policy proposal than an underlying attitude, one that informs and influences most of Dean's policies.

"One reason I am running for president is to restore the ideal of the American community," he says, an ideal he claims is "under assault" by the Bush administration.

"We seek an America where it is not enough that our own children have health care and good schools, but where our neighbors' children do as well," he says, echoing Bill Clinton's "one America" theme. "The biggest lie that people like me tell people like you is, 'Elect me and I'll solve all your problems,'" Dean says. "You have the power," he tells the voters, implying that they also have the responsibility.

UNION SUPPORTER

If Dean has taken a left-of-center position on any issue in this campaign, it is a relic of old-fashioned liberalism: He has been unabashedly pro-union.

"It was the rise of the trade union that gave our country the biggest middle class in the world," he says. "Unions have secured basic rights to health care, occupational safety and retirement protection. It is the absence of labor unions in many Third World countries that has caused the hemorrhaging of manufacturing jobs from U.S.-based factories to offshore plants."

It isn't that Dean seeks radical changes to the labor laws. His proposals are less sweeping than the labor law reforms promoted unsuccessfully by Jimmy Carter in the 1970s. They include new civil penalties for employers who refuse to bargain in good faith, automatic recognition of a union when a majority of the work force has signed membership cards, and a ban on one-on-one anti-union meetings. But the implications are clear: Here Dean endorses the downward income redistribution he rejects in his tax policies. Reluctant to have government lead the way toward greater equality through the tax code, Dean wants to encourage the private sector to accomplish the same task through stronger labor unions.

HEALTH CARE, EDUCATION

Similarly, Dean's health care plan — a combination of tax incentives to business, tax credits to middle-income individuals and direct government support for health insurance for lower-income people — is less sweeping than the one Bill Clinton promoted unsuccessfully in the 1990s. Dean would cover all kids and young adults up to age 25, extend eligibility for the Children's Health Insurance Program to all households earning up to 185 percent of the poverty level, establish a new "affordable health insurance plan people can buy into" similar to the plan covering Congress and federal workers, and offer more tax benefits to corporations that provide health care coverage for their workers.

Dean claims that his health plan would cost $88.9 billion a year and would cover an additional 28.8 million people. It would not, then, cover everyone. All Americans would be eligible, but some could opt out, and the Dean campaign estimates that roughly 10 million people would do so. Still, if it worked, coverage would approach the 92 percent (96 percent of all children) covered in Vermont. Dean's health care claim is similar to his budget-balancing claim: If he did it in Vermont, he can do it nationwide.

When it comes to education, Dean wants to undo what George Bush has done. Many Democrats in Congress, including liberals such as Sen. Edward Kennedy of Massachusetts, ended up supporting Bush's No Child Left Behind Act, which requires all third- through eighth-graders to be tested and imposes penalties on schools that do not meet "adequate yearly progress" targets. Looking at it from the perspective of a governor who had dealt with education at the grass roots for a decade, Dean opposed it.

"It's a huge unfunded mandate, and it turns out not to be very good education policy, either," he says. "It's the problem with one-size-fits-all. It's really harming the majority of schools all over the country."

Dean would replace the Bush plan with a more flexible system. "I'd have a national test," he says, "national standards, and very high standards. But what the sanctions would be would be up to the states and localities. We'd provide technical assistance to help those schools that are in real trouble. And all the tests would be fully paid for, and there would be no unfunded mandates."

Again relying on his experience as governor, Dean says, "The standards that they have are wholly unrealistic. It's as though they never talked to a local school board or superintendent. I have."

FOREIGN POLICY AND DEFENSE

But what he did as governor is irrelevant to one vital presidential responsibility: foreign and defense policy. As his opponents often note, governors play no part in international affairs, and because his candidacy caught fire after he opposed President Bush over the war in Iraq, he is in danger of being pictured as a foreign policy naïf.

He disagrees. "Look, I've been in more than 50 countries, which is more than the president of the United States will have been in by next November," he says. "I have more foreign policy experience than Ronald Reagan or George W. Bush did when they took over the presidency."

Actually, he has exactly as much foreign policy experience as they had: none. It is true that Dean had more curiosity than Bush about the world outside the United States. Though he was single and wealthy for a decade, George W. Bush never left the country as a young adult, whereas Dean traveled extensively. But walking around Paris, or even living in England for a while as Dean did, is not foreign policy experience. Neither is heading a trade delegation to drum up business for your state. No matter what they say, governors do not do foreign policy.

Presidential hopeful Howard Dean plays his guitar during a jam session on August 14, 2003, in Des Moines, Iowa.
(AP Photo by Charlie Neibergall)

Politically, George W. Bush had some foreign policy cover in 2000; he was his father's son and campaigned with his father's foreign and defense officials, including Colin Powell. That gave voters some idea of what his policies would be.

Dean has no comparable national security all-star supporting cast. The foreign policy experts he has consulted, according to his campaign, include former Secretary of State Madeleine Albright, former national security adviser Sandy Berger, retired Gen. Wesley Clark and retired Marine Corps Gen. Joseph Hoar, the former commander in chief of U.S. Central Command. Unfortunately for Dean, Hoar, the least-known of these, is the only one who has endorsed him. Clark is now running against him.

Still, this list of advisers provides some insight into what Dean's foreign and defense policies would be. They would be mainstream Democratic, not unlike Bill Clinton's. A President Dean would be far less likely than President Bush to abrogate treaties, send troops to fight without U.N. approval, or accept the kind of rift with European allies that accompanied the decision to go to war in Iraq. Dean is a committed multilateralist.

He would not, however, be unalterably opposed to military action. Albright, in particular, was known as one of the Clinton administration officials most willing to use force, not just to protect American interests but sometimes to assert American values. "What's the point of having this superb military you're always talking about if we can't use it?" she once asked Powell, then chairman of the Joint Chiefs of Staff, when she did and he did not want to intervene in Bosnia. Powell later wrote, "I thought I would have an aneurysm."

Dean's approach would be closer to Albright's than to Powell's. He often cites her description of the United States as the world's "indispensable power."

"My defense policy is that I think we have the right to strike anybody in self-defense," Dean says. "We have a right to stop attacks, and we have an obligation to intervene in cases of genocide with other world bodies, with the U.N. and NATO."

Even on Iraq, Dean was not totally opposed to military action to remove Saddam Hussein from power. "What I said from the beginning is that Saddam should be removed by U.N. forces. And in the meantime, we should contain him," he says. What he opposed was what he called (not quite correctly) a "unilateral war," without the sanction of the United Nations.

"I am not a pacifist. I believe there are times when pre-emptive force is justified, but there has to be an immediate threat, and there just wasn't in this case," Dean says.

While Dean would not have gotten U.S. forces into Iraq when and how Bush did, he wouldn't take them right out, either. Instead, he would replace some American troops with about

100,000 "NATO and U.N. troops, preferably including some Arab speakers, perhaps from Egypt and Morocco." These foreign forces, he says, would not have command over American troops. "It would require giving up our command over the occupation, but not over American troops," he says.

"I'd like to bring our Guard and reserve troops home and change the rotation schedule," he says. As to how long the occupation would last, he says, "There is no way of knowing that. Ten years, maybe longer. Chaos is much more dangerous than Saddam Hussein. Chaos is good for al-Qaida."

Dean also wants more troops — but not Americans — in Afghanistan, which he called another Bush administration foreign policy failure. He says the United States should "increase to 30,000–40,000 the number of military troops our friends and allies commit to help us rebuild." The Bush policy, he says, relies "on warlords to keep the peace in Afghanistan," demonstrating "an extraordinary lack of thoughtful vision."

Nor is Dean in favor of spending less on national security.

"I don't think we can cut the defense budget," he says. "We're not paying for adequate homeland security. Twenty percent of American soldiers get food stamps, and the Bush administration is cutting pay for soldiers in hazardous duty."

When he said that in a late-summer interview, the Bush administration had just decided not to cut hazardous-duty pay, though it was still intent on cutting veterans benefits, which Dean also opposes.

"This doesn't mean we can't realign spending," Dean says. Dismissing Bush's strategic defense program with its old Reagan-era nickname, "Star Wars," Dean says he would continue missile defense research, but at the very least hold off on deployment until scientists were certain the system would be effective.

But — again like Eisenhower, who often rejected the Pentagon's hard-line recommendations and who closed his presidency warning about the dangers of the "military-industrial complex" — Dean as president would not grant the Pentagon all it wished, either in equipment or in policy. By the summer of

2003, Dean was talking about how a president sometimes has to stand up to the hawks in his own administration. During the Cuban Missile Crisis, Dean says, "President Kennedy took on the hawks among the Joint Chiefs of Staff as well as the 'me-too'ers' in Congress. The president and his advisers used toughness, patience and diplomacy. The missiles came out of Cuba and war was averted."

Were he president now, Dean would take on Pentagon hard-liners over at least three issues: He

> "Israel has always been a longtime ally with a special relationship with the United States. But, if we are going to bargain by being in the middle of the negotiations, then we are going to have to take an evenhanded role."
>
> *Howard Dean,*
> *2003 Interview*

would revive the Anti-ballistic Missile Treaty with the Russians from which Bush withdrew; he would sign the treaty banning land mines that President Clinton refused to accept; and he would begin bilateral talks with North Korea over its nuclear program, a step the Bush administration has refused to take, arguing that it would "reward" North Korea for its nuclear ambitions.

"The president has really messed that up," Dean says in an interview, accusing Bush of "petulance" over Korea.

From a historical perspective, the defense debate seems more political and symbolic than substantive. At least since World War II, no American president has allowed the country's military strength to decline, and it is implausible that any president ever would, even if he could. People do not seek power in order to diminish it, and nothing makes a president of the United States stronger than the nation's military might. In the 2000 presidential campaign, Republicans complained that President Clinton had allowed the armed forces to deteriorate. But those were largely Bill Clinton's armed forces that won the battles in Afghanistan and Iraq.

There are legitimate debates over specific weapons systems, treaties and strategies. But despite the rhetoric that often accompanies them, neither side intends to end up with a weaker military force. However these debates are resolved, in the final analysis all presidents maintain, indeed enhance, the power of the armed forces. They really have no choice.

But Dean's insistence on a high level of defense spending does divide him from the left wing of his party.

"It is not progressive to say the Pentagon budget is off-limits to cuts," Jeff Cohen, the spokesman for Rep. Dennis Kucinich of Ohio, one of Dean's opponents for the nomination, told the *Village Voice*. "It's not progressive to say that you want more troops in Iraq, and that we're stuck there. It's not progressive to say the embargo on Cuba, which is an absurd policy which persisted for decades, should continue."

Dean, who in the past has criticized the Cuban embargo, now says it should not be lifted lest the step be seen as approval of the recent harsh sentences for various crimes and other draconian policies of Fidel Castro's government.

MIDDLE EAST

Dean also breaks with the foreign policy left over the Middle East. Like most liberals and many conservatives, he supports a "two-state solution" to the Israeli-Palestinian dispute. But he says, "It would be very hard to pressure the Israelis [to dismantle their West Bank settlements] while they're being killed by terrorists." When the suicide bombings cease, he says, he would "pressure both sides" to reach an agreement.

Dean stumbled into a small political thicket in September 2003 when he told a New Mexico audience that an "enormous number" of Israeli settlements on the West Bank would have to be dismantled as part of any peace accord, and that it was not America's place "to take sides" in the conflict. The Dean campaign quickly explained that he meant only that America should not take sides on the specific negotiating details between the two sides.

"Israel has always been a longtime ally with a special relationship with the United States," Dean says. "But if we are going to bargain by being in the middle of the negotiations then we are going to have to take an evenhanded role."

For all the tumult Dean's remarks caused, fundamental support for Israel is as much a presidential obligation as keeping the country strong. Parties and candidates may differ over timetables, details and personalities, but there is a foreign policy consensus behind America's commitment to the security of the state of Israel — based on strategic and moral, as well as political, considerations. Dean has always been part of that consensus, which now includes support for a Palestinian state. This is one area where Howard Dean and George W. Bush agree.

Though Dean never comes close to the rhapsodic veneration of the Palestinian cause demanded by the left, he regularly praises the Palestinian people.

"The Palestinians have assets that are often misunderstood," he says. "They have a high level of education. Palestinian women play a more significant role in government than in almost any other Arab society. And a large number of Palestinians have a significant experience with democracy, having lived in Europe, the United States and, of course, in Israel."

Significantly, though, Dean admires the Palestinians for their modernity and their moderation, not their revolutionary zeal. "Yasser Arafat is not the answer," he makes clear, mentioning instead the names of moderate Palestinian leaders.

But like many other Democrats, Dean refuses to allow the Middle East to remain solely a foreign policy issue. He brings it home.

"The United States must reduce its dependence on Middle Eastern oil, and we must have a president who is willing to confront the Iranians, the Syrians, the Saudis and others who send money to Hamas and finance a worldwide network of fundamentalist schools which teach small children to hate Americans, Christians and Jews," he says.

ALTERNATIVE ENERGY

Howard Dean's Middle East policy, then, includes windmills. It is both a foreign and a domestic policy, based on making the United States less dependent on foreign oil by increasing production of renewable (and non-polluting) energy, primarily wind, solar energy and ethanol. The intent here is to diminish both the clout of Saudi Arabia and the greenhouse gas emissions that cause global warming.

"This is no Birkenstock Vermont liberal crazy idea," he tells audiences. "Denmark gets 20 percent of its energy from wind power."

In fact it is running at 19 percent this year, according to Linette Riis of the Danish Windturbine Owners Association, emitting 3.4 million fewer tons of carbon dioxide into the northern European air. Dean appears to be right when he says that developing wind power would reduce both the amount of oil imported and climate change. What Dean does not mention is that while wind power may be popular in Denmark, it is controversial even in Vermont, where many of his former constituents fear the tall towers will ruin the mountaintop scenery. Dean finesses this point. The windmills, he suggests, should be concentrated on the Great Plains.

Like many politicians seeking support in Iowa, Dean also supports increased use of ethanol, the clean-burning but controversial fuel additive extracted from corn. "If you had 10 percent ethanol in everybody's gas tank in this country, you would reduce oil use by 5 percent," he says.

Requiring more ethanol in auto fuel is popular in the Farm Belt. It is unpopular with many economists and engineers who argue that it takes almost as many BTUs to produce a pound of ethanol as that pound provides and that the entire ethanol experiment is economically feasible only because of tax subsidies.

But it takes BTUs to produce coal, oil, natural gas and nuclear energy, too, and they also get tax preferences. About 40 percent of the cars in Brazil operate on 100 percent ethanol, according to the Renewable Fuels Association, the lobby for the wind, solar and biomass energy industries, with the rest running on a blend of mostly ethanol. Clearly the potential exists for the United States to burn more ethanol, should it choose.

Considering Dean's concern about global warming, it is no surprise that he would reverse Bush's unilateral withdrawal from the Kyoto treaty designed to reduce greenhouse gases. But it's something of a surprise that he opposes the treaty as written.

"The U.S. should find a way to sign it, but we can't yet," he said during a radio interview in March. "It is a flawed treaty because it doesn't require the underdeveloped countries to do anything about greenhouse gases, particularly Brazil and China. And what I would have done with Kyoto is not what the president did. . . . I would like to find a way to sign it, and that means renegotiating the piece with the underdeveloped countries that would also require them to reduce greenhouse gases over a much longer time period."

FOREIGN TRADE

Kyoto is not the only treaty Dean would renegotiate. He also wants to get the rest of the world back to the bargaining table to redo the two major trade initiatives — the North America Free Trade Agreement and the World Trade Organization Treaties — inserting new protections for the rights of workers and the environment.

"Trade is a good thing," he told a New Hampshire audience, "but our trade agreements need to be renegotiated. All our trade agreements need to include labor standards, child labor protections, a guarantee of the right [of workers] to organize, and environmental protections."

Asked how he could persuade other countries to renegotiate the trade agreements, Dean says simply, "We're not obligated to take in their goods." In short, he would get tough, saying to other nations: "If you want to sell your goods in the United States, you'll have to do it on our terms." But having pushed for treaties without labor and environmental safeguards, the United States risks being painted as a bully, and a fickle bully at that, if it were to demand that the rest of the world rewrite the treaties.

And there is something close to a mainstream consensus that more trade benefits everyone. Adoption of the trade agreements in 1994 and 1995 was followed by strong economic growth, the creation of millions of new jobs and expanded international trade leading to lower-priced goods. If nothing else, tougher trade standards could result in higher prices.

Howard Dean shares a laugh with *Tonight Show* host Jay Leno on September 30, 2003. *(AP Photo by Reed Saxon)*

"One could argue that the American labor movement raised the price of goods," Dean says, when asked about the likely consequences of his proposal. In an earlier interview with *Slate* magazine, he was even more blunt when asked whether his plan would raise the price of goods: "Yeah," he said. "But so what? Because in return for making the price of goods go up, you've fixed the illegal immigration problem, you've fixed the drain of jobs problem, you've created a middle class that can buy American exports. There's a lot you get for that."

Here, finally, for those seeking him, is Howard Dean the radical, breaking not just with the Bush Republicans but with the establishment consensus that included the Clinton Democrats. It was an unpopular consensus, a good example of how American democracy often responds to well-placed elites, not the majority of the voters. Polls leave little doubt that most people oppose "free trade," perhaps knowing that there is nothing free about it. Were it free, the trade treaties would be brief — "you can send your stuff here; we can send our stuff there" — instead of taking up hundreds of pages of rules and regulations, most of them protecting the interests of investors, lenders and manufacturers — the very elites molding the pro-trade consensus. In government, in the academic world and among the journalistic upper echelon, it was and remains gauche to question the wisdom of "free trade."

Dean dares to be gauche. The pro-trade establishment insists that less is more — that low prices, low wages and low taxes bring economic growth, lots of jobs, enough prosperity for all and boundless opportunities for some. Seen in the context of his labor and tax policies, Dean's trade proposal indicates that he thinks less can be less and more is often more, that this would be a healthier society if more workers here and abroad earned higher wages, even if that meant they'd have to pay a bit more for goods and send a little more to the government.

But by now "free trade" may have become as much a part of the American political wallpaper as a strong defense and support for Israel. Even a Democratic president backed by a strongly Democratic Congress (which few predict from the 2004 election) would have a hard time slipping a plan to renegotiate the internationl trade agreements past the barricades that would be erected by lobbyists, editorial writers and an aroused corporate community.

Perhaps because they are aware of these political and economic realities, Dean's campaign advisers warn that his proposals should be interpreted broadly, that he is dealing in "nuance," and that his intent is not to scuttle existing agreements but to "put the world on notice that the interests of the middle class and laboring folks" are as important as those of corporations.

They are not quite saying, "Howard is oversimplifying the issue to get union leaders' support; the actual policy would be subtler," but they're coming close. This is not an unprecedented tactic in American politics. Nor does it mean that Dean's proposal is either insincere or insubstantial. This appears to be a case in which the proclaimed policy indicates a general direction but does not predict specific legislation. If the United States used its market power to support the interests of workers and environmental protection, the trade pacts would probably be enforced and interpreted differently, even if unchanged.

FARM ISSUES

Dean takes an equally populist line when it comes to rural and agricultural matters, proposing to change farm programs so they benefit the family farmer, not corporate agribusiness. He wants to "reduce the amount of federal subsidies to corporate megafarms" and has pledged to use the antitrust laws to control concentration of the meat- and grain-processing industries.

He also pledged to try to close a "loophole passed by Republicans in 2002" that he says allows "large, corporate concentrated animal feeding operations to receive millions in government aid while skirting environmental rules" and "to institute a national packer ban, ensuring meatpackers cannot own livestock prior to slaughter."

These are similar to proposals that most Democratic and some Republican presidential candidates have made for years, decades in some cases, without slowing the process by which agriculture becomes increasingly dominated by fewer, larger farms selling their products to a handful of concentrated corporate processors. Dean insists it is not too late to save the family farm and the rural towns those farms support.

WORK IN PROGRESS

Like the rest of his candidacy, Howard Dean's policies are a work in progress. Dean has been in government for 15 years and is generally familiar with the national debates over most of the issues a president faces. But the decisions of any governor do not affect the nation's economy, its armed forces, its natural resources or its social cohesion to any measurable extent. As did Reagan, Clinton and George W. Bush before him, Dean is learning as he runs. As did they, he makes some mistakes.

One mistake he hopes not to make is to promise more than he can deliver. Wearing his budget-balancing obsession proudly, he says he wants to make sure he does not propose more government spending than his tax structure can finance. For a while, his staff was crunching the numbers to make sure that rescinding the Bush tax cuts would pay for all of

Dean's proposals and balance the budget to boot.

Then came that August 2003 CBO report showing that the year's deficit and the long-term budget imbalance would be far larger than previous estimates indicated. By mid-September Dean was still insisting that the budget would be balanced but acknowledging that "it will take awhile."

Still, he insists that a Dean administration "will provide health care, and we will provide prescription drugs for seniors, and we will provide other services to the middle class that this president has destroyed. But we will do it with a balanced budget." Truman would have admired that. So would have Ike.

Jon Margolis

FROM THE CARTOONISTS

"HE'S HERE, TOO! EVERYWHERE YOU LOOK THIS SUMMER IT'S HOWARD DEAN!"

The Early Years

Vermont Governor Howard Dean learned many a valuable lesson about hard work and Yankee frugality on those frosty mornings when chores had to be done before the long trip to school...

PAN AM

313 PARK AVE

DANZIGER

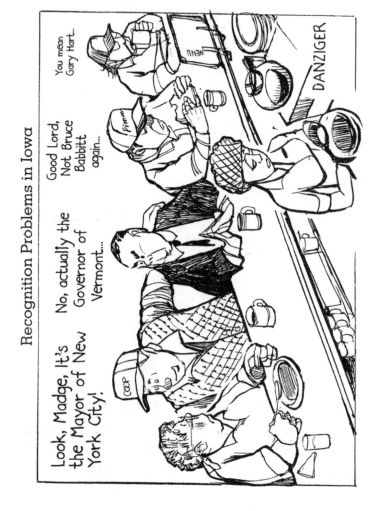

Problems of an Ex-Vermont Governor Campaigning in New Hampshire

A snowy January day in 2002 at the
Statehouse in Montpelier.
(Times-Argus *Photo*)

The Reporters

DARREN ALLEN is chief of the Vermont Press Bureau, the Statehouse bureau of the *Rutland Herald* and the *Barre-Montpelier Times-Argus*. A journalist since 1987, Allen has covered politics, legal affairs and finance. He has worked for the *Baltimore Sun,* the *Sun-Sentinel* of South Florida and the *Intelligencer Journal* of Lancaster, Pennsylvania. He also worked for the Bureau of National Affairs Inc., where he wrote about taxation issues. He holds a degree from Northwestern University's Medill School of Journalism and lives in Montpelier, Vermont.

MARK BUSHNELL is a freelance writer and former reporter and editor for the *Sunday Rutland Herald* and *Times-Argus*. His history column, *Life in the Past Lane,* runs in *Vermont Sunday Magazine,* a weekly publication of the *Herald* and *Times-Argus.* He is a graduate of Middlebury College and lives in Middlesex, Vermont.

HAMILTON E. DAVIS is a former Washington, D.C., bureau chief for the *Providence Journal* and is a former managing editor of the *Burlington Free Press*. As a Washington reporter, he covered the 1968 and 1972 presidential elections. In addition to freelance writing, he is a health policy analyst and a research associate of the University of Vermont College of Medicine. He has served in several posts in the executive and legislative branches of Vermont state government. He is the author of *Mocking Justice* (Crown Publishers, 1978), a book about a drug scandal in Vermont. He lives in Burlington, Vermont.

JOHN DILLON is a reporter for Vermont Public Radio, where he covers the Howard Dean presidential campaign, among other assignments. A veteran Vermont journalist, Dillon also has worked for the *Sunday Rutland Herald* and *Times-Argus,* United

Press International, and columnist Jack Anderson in Washington, D.C. He was educated at the University of Vermont, and in 1995–96 he attended the Massachusetts Institute of Technology as a Knight Science Journalism Fellow. His work has appeared on National Public Radio, and he has freelanced for *Vermont Life* magazine, the *Boston Globe,* the *New York Times* and *Audubon Magazine.* He lives in Middlesex, Vermont.

DAVID GRAM has been a reporter in the Vermont bureau of the Associated Press in Montpelier since 1985, save for the 1995–96 academic year, when he won a Kiplinger Fellowship at Ohio State University. He earned a bachelor's degree at the University of Massachusetts at Amherst and a master's degree at Ohio State University. As an AP reporter, Gram has covered Howard Dean, the Vermont legislature and a host of topics ranging from energy to religion. He lives in Montpelier, Vermont.

SALLY WEST JOHNSON is a freelance writer and former reporter and editor for the *Rutland Herald.* She worked for the *Associated Press* and *Newsweek* in New York and was the editor of *Vermont Sunday Magazine,* a weekly publication of the *Herald* and *Times-Argus.* She also was editor of *Vermont Magazine,* a bimonthly publication. She is a graduate of Middlebury College and lives in Middlebury, Vermont.

JON MARGOLIS covered presidential campaigns from 1968 through 1996 for *Newsday* and the *Chicago Tribune.* He is the author of three books, most recently *The Last Innocent Year: America in 1964* (William Morrow, 1999). He is a graduate of Oberlin College and has written for *Esquire,* the *New Republic,* the *American Prospect* and the *New York Times Sunday Magazine.* He lives in Barton, Vermont.

DAVID MOATS is editorial page editor of the *Rutland Herald.* He is a graduate of the University of California at Santa Barbara. He won the 2001 Pulitzer Prize for editorial writing and is the author of the forthcoming book *Civil Wars: Gay Marriage Puts Democracy to the Test* (Harcourt, 2004). He lives in Middlebury, Vermont.

IRENE WIELAWSKI is a freelance journalist who writes primarily on health care topics for national publications. For more than 20 years she was a staff writer for daily newspapers, including the *Burlington Free Press,* the *Providence Journal* and the *Los Angeles Times.* She was a Pulitzer Prize finalist for specialized reporting (medicine) while at the *Journal* and was a member of the special investigations team at the *Los Angeles Times.* She is a graduate of Vassar College and lives in Pound Ridge, New York.

OTHER CONTRIBUTORS
Cartoonists: Jeff Danziger and Tim Newcomb
Production directors: Anita Ancel
Photo/Design editor: Jeb Wallace-Brodeur
Chief copy editor: Ruth Hare
Copy editors: Mark Bushnell, Anne Galloway, Heather Stephenson and Steve Wallach
Design and layout assistant: Tammy Hooker
Researcher: Eric Francis